Reader Comments
(from the blog this book is based on)

◆**I wish I would have read your blog before I published my first novel with Outskirts.** I have had some scathing reviews due to the errors that were left in my book after I paid a small fortune for editing with the Outskirts editing team. I tried to reason with my so-called marketing representative, but she simply hid behind the "fine print" they give you *after* they receive payment from you.

◆OH MY GOSH! This just gets better and better. HA HA HA!! wait, let me pause and take a breath. HA HA HA HA! God, this blog is always good for a laugh. And you can't make this shit up, folks. Truth really IS stranger than fiction. Michael — you are fearless. **You've got a pair of brass ones. These bastards are going to sue you** one day, I'm telling you. But you'd probably be tickled pink... more publicity for you!

◆Brent's revisionist history of the use of the "self-publishing" term by vanity publishers is blatant bullshit. **You kicked his ass and revealed, once again, that Brent is either an ignorant fool or a deliberate liar** — and neither is good for a publisher.

◆Michael, **you are brave indeed**. I must admit, much braver than I am.

◆ENOUGH trash talk! Stop picking on them! You should honor Outskirts Press, not condemn them. Outskirts Press should be commended for being socially responsible. **They hire editors who are mentally handicapped or blind, or both**.

The author's blogs:

◆**Book Making** is where Michael discusses writing, editing and publishing — for writers and readers.
http://BookMakingBlog.blogspot.com
◆**Become a Real Self-Publisher** is the online companion to the book by the same name. It's the repository for additions, corrections and comments.
http://Real-Self-Publisher.blogspot.com
◆**For The First Time (or the last time)** talks about changes in society and technology: first toilet paper, last country to get TV, first voicemail, last Automat, first female Boy Scout leader.
http://4TheFirstTime.blogspot.com
◆**Oh How Stupid** provides an occasional look at some of the stupidest things done by human beings.
http://OhHowStupid.blogspot.com
◆**Letters to April Wong** is a collection of stupid and scam emails sent to a person who does not exist.
http://LettersToAprilWong.blogspot.com
◆**Gotta Get One** recommends and criticizes electronics, cars, cameras, tools, movies, food, books and more.
http://GottaGet1.blogspot.com
◆**911 Wackos.** Some folks call 911 for strange reasons. Sometimes they get into trouble after the call. Sometimes the 911 operators get into trouble. http://911Wackos.blogspot.com
◆**Dial Zero** provides a look at what's silly, stupid or surprising in telecom. http://DialZero.blogspot.com

His other books:

◆CB Bible (co-author, 1976)
◆What Phone System Should I Buy? (1996)
◆I Only Flunk My Brightest Students (2008)
◆Phone Systems & Phones for Small Business & Home (2009)
◆The AbleComm Guide to Phone Systems (2009)
◆Telecom Reference eBook (2009)
◆Become a <u>Real</u> Self-Publisher (2010)
◆Stories I'd Tell My Children (2010)
◆The 100 Worst Self-Publishing Misteaks (co-author, 2010)

Stupid, Sloppy, Sleazy

The Strange Story of Vanity Publisher Outskirts Press. How do they stay in business?

◆

Michael N. Marcus

SILVER SANDS BOOKS

www.SilverSandsBooks.com
230 Woodmont Road, Suite 15
Milford CT 06460
books@ablecomm.com
203.878.8383

Library of Congress Control Number: 2010902917
ISBN: 978-0-9816617-2-8 (for pBook)
Version 1.36 (CS-9/LL-7)

◆This book was published to provide information quickly and at minimum cost. It's also an experiment in using CreateSpace and Lulu. The book was not professionally edited or designed (normally terrible sins) and the author apologizes for the esthetic limitations and any uncorrected errors. This is the 36th version of the book. The next version will be better.

◆ Please use the physical or email addresses on the previous page for corrections, questions or comments.

◆This book is adapted from postings on BookMakingBlog.blogspot.com. Some chapters were published in *Become a Real Self-Publisher: Don't be a Victim of a Vanity Press.*

Contents

Author's notes   9

Introduction   10

Chapter 1   17
This publisher needs an editor

Chapter 2   19
Publishing company with editing trouble
needs help with math, too

Chapter 3   21
More BS from Brent Sampson

Chapter 4   27
More Picking on Outskirts Press

Chapter 5   29
A challenge to Outskirts Press:
prove you're not full of crap

Chapter 6   31
$30,000 book royalties in one month?
It's time to pick on Outskirts Press again.

Chapter 7   35
More lies from Outskirts Press

Chapter 8   41
More incompetence from Outskirts Press

Chapter 9   45
Outskirts Press keeps getting stupider

Chapter 10   47
Stupid and cheap Outskirts Press helps competitors

Chapter 11   51
Outskirts Press idiots show how NOT to write a press release

Chapter 12   59
An Outskirts victim speaks: Outskirts Press editing is like "no editing at all."

Chapter 13   61
NO SURPRISE: The Outskirts Press contract avoids responsibility for errors and has a stupid typo. BIG SURPRISE: authors might loan Outskirts money for six months, interest-free!

Chapter 14   65
OMG. Outskirts Press actually paid money to distribute a press release. What's next: a cure for the common cold, or peace in the Middle-East?

Chapter 15   69
Pathetically stupid Outskirts Press misspelled its own name and helps its competitors

Chapter 16   71
Save up to $199. Write your own Outskirts Press press release

Chapter 17   75
Suffering from ED? Outskirts idiots misspell their own name again.

Chapter 18   77
Michael and Brent debate (sort of)

Chapter 19   91
I'm not sure if Outskirts Press is cheating or stupid, but I know it's lying.

Chapter 20   95
It doesn't get much better than this:
Vanity publisher Outskirts Press brags about its
vanity award from a scam organization

Chapter 21   101
Are key employees at Outskirts Press trying to
find new jobs?

Chapter 22   103
Reality Check: Outskirts Press distribution vs.
real self-publishing

Chapter 23   107
OMG, another brain fart from Brent Sampson

Chapter 24   109
OMG, another complaint from an Outskirts author

Chapter 25   111
Why am I so damned critical?

Chapter 26   115
What would Jesus think?

Chapter 27   117
It's not just Outskirts

Chapter 28   119
Sifting through the BS:
What is "real" self-publishing?

Chapter 29   129
Editors and Editing

About the author   133

> "To exceed the expectations of every author we help publish."
>
> –Outskirts Press Mission Statement:
>
>
>
> "Outskirts made me feel paranoid about not getting their editing service, but when I did it was as if I had no editing at all."
>
> –Outskirts Press Author

Author's notes

So, how *does* Outskirts Press stay in business?

By attracting writers who know even less about publishing than the employees and management of Outskirts Press know.

I am not a competitor of Outskirts Press.

I have nothing to lose or gain if people don't do business with Outskirts Press — and nothing to lose or gain if people *do* do business with Outskirts Press. I am an observer, not a participant.

I'd rather convince Outskirts Press to "clean up its act," than convince people not to use its services.

People at Outskirts Press have refused to respond to my emails, even those asking very simple questions.

◆

In the two years I've been aware of Outskirts Press, my opinion of the company and Brent Sampson, its founder and boss, has been overwhelmingly negative. I have frequently found him to be deceptive and incompetent.

As I was nearing completion of this book, I heard Brent interviewed on BlogTalkRadio.com. Brent was putting his best foot forward and may have been acting, but he seemed articulate, knowledgeable, honest and even humble. I felt he was both less sinister and less stupid than his print persona.

Maybe this publisher should stick to verbal — not textual — communication. I'd think more of him if I had never read anything he wrote.

MNM

Introduction

Outskirts Press, Inc., located on the outskirts of Denver, Colorado, describes itself as "the fastest-growing full-service publishing provider." It published just seven books in 2002, its first year, and over 5,000 books in 2009.

Despite that impressive growth, the company often seems to be deliberately dishonest and hopelessly inept.

◆Outskirts misleads potential author-customers, overcharges for products and services, and staff members hide behind contractual fine print when errors occur.

◆Outskirts makes many stupid mistakes in publishing and publicizing its authors' books.

◆Outskirts even makes stupid mistakes while promoting *itself* online and in print.

Despite its use of many labels (e.g., "self-publishing," "custom book publishing," "print-on-demand publishing," "independent self-printing") the company is a *vanity publisher*. Vanity publishers appeal to the desire of starry-eyed writers to become "published authors" despite poor writing skills or topics with limited appeal.

Traditional publishers try to make money by selling books to readers. Vanity publishers sell some books to readers, but the bulk of their income comes from selling services to naïve and misinformed writers.

Outskirts' customers pay up to $1099 for publishing packages which include up to 10 "free books" that are actually paid for. The company encourages customers to buy highly profitable, overpriced trinkets ranging from 40-cent business cards to promotional postage stamps which cost nearly three times the value of the postage.

The company also sells overpriced services, such as copyright registration for $99 (an author can register for $35), and contest submission for $299 (an author can enter the contest for $180 plus the cost of a few books).

Why does this book exist?

1. To make potential Outskirts Press customers (and potential customers of other vanity publishers) aware of the trouble that likely awaits them.
2. To encourage writers to be very careful about picking publishers.
3. To let dishonest and incompetent publishers know that they are being watched.

A small business with a huge ego

Outskirts Press says it's "press release happy" and "We try to distribute [press releases] every Tuesday." Outskirts loves to publicize awards — even dubious awards (next page).

According to the company, in both 2007 and 2008 *The Denver Business Journal* recognized Outskirts as the fastest-growing publisher, and the fastest-growing privately held "small-to-medium" sized company in Colorado, with growth of over 500% for 2005-2007.

In 2009, *Inc* magazine named Outskirts Press to its annual "Inc 500" list of the nation's fastest-growing businesses. The ranking is based on the rate of revenue growth from 2005 through 2008, when Outskirts claims it grew by 850.5%.

Outskirts is the 21st fastest-growing business in the Consumer Products & Services category on the *Inc* list. (Some people question whether a book publisher provides *consumer* products and services, since an author who uses its services is engaged in a *business*, and many Outskirts books are aimed at businesses.)

Also in 2009, Outskirts issued a press release that said, "Outskirts Press, Inc. Receives 2009 Best of Business Award. Small Business Commerce Association's Award Honors the Achievement." The release did not say that the award was given by a company that makes money by selling award trophies and plaques, and has been sanctioned by the Better Business Bureau. The vanity publisher was bragging about a *vanity award* also given to a tattoo remover and a bagpipe player.

The boss

Outskirts Press was started in 2002 by Brent Sampson  "after several frustrating attempts at traditional publication." *Celebrity Parents* magazine said that before Brent decided to self-publish, he received "many rejection letters (which he's now proud of)." That's pathetic. Why is Brent proud of failure? And why is Brent considered a celebrity?

His first book, *The Art of Poetry*, is a collection of illustrated poems published by vanity publisher iUniverse. Despite over eight years of availability, there is *not even one* review for that book on Amazon.com. Its sales rank has been below 7,000,000 — making it one of Amazon's worst sellers.

Brent is Outskirts' Chief Executive Officer and Chief Marketing Officer. He says he has degrees in English and film from the University of Colorado, and calls himself "an accomplished artist and writer." Because of his degree in English and his position as head of a publishing company, the mistakes in his writing are unforgiveable.

The company

Despite pretensions of grandeur, Outskirts Press seems to be a home-based "mom-and-pop" business. **The corporate address is Mailbox #515 in a UPS store** in Parker, Colorado ("behind McDonald's"). Outskirts may have as few as three full-time employees, plus freelancers with varying levels of skill, education and experience.

The clan

Outskirts Press is a family business. **Brent Sampson** is CEO and CMO. **Lynn Sampson** (presumably Brent's sister, sister-in-law or cousin) is CFO and CTO. Brent's wife, **Jeanine Laiza Sampson**, is COO. The Better Business Bureau lists **Bruce Sampson** as "additional company management personnel," but his name could not be found on the company's website. **Tony Sampson**'s Facebook page displays an Outskirts Press email address, but he lives in Florida and may not be involved in the company. Tony misspelled "independent" on Facebook.

Lynn "oversees...all the financial management" and is an attorney. She seems to be tough. Your book can be canceled if you owe Outskirts $25 for 31 days, even while they owe you thousands of dollars in royalties.

Jeanine's name appears on some horrid press releases. Like Brent, she apparently has a degree in English. Before joining Outskirts she worked as an interior designer. Jeanine "oversees over 100 book production professionals," but they probably don't actually work at Outskirts.

Total Outskirts employment is difficult to determine.

Based on info provided by Outskirts, the profile published by *Inc* magazine in 2009 said that Outskirts has just three employees. Only Brent, Jeanine and Lynn are shown on the Outskirts website. Wikipedia reported that the company uses about 150 contractors (i.e., freelancers) as of July 2007. Linkedin.com said that Outskirts had 25 employees. Manta.com said that Outskirts "employs a staff of approximately 1-4." Cortera.com said that Outskirts employs five to ten people.

Two non-Sampsons were known to work for Outskirts as of March, 2010 — but they may be freelancing. **Kelly Schuknecht** is Director of Author Support, and her name goes on most of the company's very poorly written press releases. Kelly's Facebook page says she lives in Spencer, Iowa. Spencer is over 700 miles from the Outskirts Press HQ, so Kelly probably doesn't commute every day. **Karl Schroeder** is Director of Author Services. He writes a blog and promotional emails for prospective customers. He is a sloppy writer, has trouble with arithmetic and won't respond to my emails.

14

Better Business Bureau complaints

The Better Business Bureau gives Outskirts Press a B+ rating and shows 38 complaints against the company (23 complaints were about poor service). The company produces some really terrible books, with bumbled promotion, and its tactics and policies upset some authors.

For comparison, the much larger Author Solutions had 73 complaints reported to the BBB. Author Solutions' sales volume is about six times that of Outskirts, but it has only about three times as many complaints.

Attraction and deception

To attract business, Outskirts brags about its "veritable army of publishing professionals" and "infrastructure of talented publishing artisans," and is frequently dishonest about other paths to publication. Outskirts tries to make independent self-publishing seem much more difficult than it really is. I corrected their chart:

	Traditional Publishing	Independent Self-Publishing	Full-Service with Outskirts Press
Wholesale distribution to Ingram and Baker & Taylor	☑	*yes!*	☑
Automatic online listings with top book retailers	☑	*yes!*	☑
Marketing support helps you sell books	☑	*yes!*	☑
Book orders are fulfilled for you	☑	*yes!*	☑
You keep all your rights		☑	☑
You control the content of your book		☑	☑
You determine how much money you make		☑	☑
You set the retail price of your book		☑	☑

From the Outskirts author contract:

"Outskirts Press does not warrant that the service or product provided will be uninterrupted or error free."

"Outskirts Press disclaims any and all representations and warranties, expressed or implied, including, without limitation, the implied warranties of merchantability, salability, or noninfringement of copyright."

In other words, don't expect Outskirts Press to do *anything* right. Based on their non-warranty, they probably should not be trusted to print toilet paper.

Chapter 1 (10/14/08)
This publisher needs an editor

Outskirts Press makes most of its money by selling services to authors, not by selling books to readers. It has called its business "custom book publishing," "on-demand publishing" and "independent self-printing." Its Google ad promotes its "Fast Easy Self Publishing," but it's really a vanity press. No company can self-publish for you. The words just don't make sense.

Its publishing packages include editing services, but the company's own publications can use better editing.

On the second page of the foreword to *Self Publishing Simplified*, Outskirts Press boss Brent Sampson refers to "off-set" printing, with a hyphen between the "off" and the "set." The term also appears on four other pages in the book.

That's a really stupid error, especially for a book publisher. The correct term is "offset," and it's been that way for over 100 years.

On his company's website, Sampson urges writers to use an editor and he says, "Errors in your writing cause readers to question your credibility." I question his.

The back-of-book bio says Sampson is an "accomplished artist and writer." His personal website has a stupid typo: "earn up to tens-of-thousands a dollars." So far I'm not impressed with his writing accomplishments.

The book has a foreword written by Sampson — which goes against book publishing tradition. The foreword is not supposed to be written by the book's author. Sampson should have called it a preface or an introduction or hired someone else to write the foreword.

According to Sampson, "Peter Mark first published the Thesaurus in 1852," strangely ignoring the much more famous Peter Roget who published *his* Thesaurus in the same year. Actually, Mark was the middle name of Peter Mark Roget, so Sampson was two-thirds right.

Roget, not Mark

He also says getting an ISBN number (the unique identification number for each book) is a "headache." Sorry, Brent, that's just not true. I ordered 10 ISBNs in about five minutes. All I needed was my keyboard and a credit card. I never touched the Tylenol bottle.

Sampson also talks about the troubles that "Most self-published authors" have getting their books distributed and the high percentages paid to Amazon. That's self-serving fiction designed to make his own company look good and he can't possibly know the experiences of "most...."

These silly errors and outright deceptions do not inspire confidence in Brent's knowledge or honesty.

Chapter 2 (10/24/08)
Publishing company with editing trouble needs help with math, too

In the first chapter I complained that a book written by the boss of Outskirts Press and the corporate website had silly errors in spelling, publishing history, book structure and more. I declared that the publisher needs an editor.

It now appears that Outskirts' employees also need a math tutor.

I received an email from one of their author services people who periodically tries to convince me to use Outskirts Press.

Karl Schroeder related an alleged conversation with a happy Outskirts author. He said, "Outskirts Press was her first choice because our authors keep all their rights. And she liked our pricing flexibility. The other publisher pays her 200% less in royalties. Yes, 200% LESS."

I'm no Einstein, but I think there's something very strange about that number.

◆To keep it simple, let's assume that Outskirts would pay a royalty of $100 for some quantity of books sold at some price over some period of time.

◆ If the other publisher paid $50, it would be 50% less than Outskirts paid.

◆ If the other publisher paid $25, it would be 75% less than Outskirts paid.

◆ If the other publisher paid absolutely nothing, it would be 100% less.

Unless there's a way to receive **less than nothing**, I can't see how it's possible to be paid 200% less than any-thing.

I asked Karl for an explanation but I didn't get it.

More BS from Brent Sampson

Brent Sampson is the founder and boss of Outskirts Press. His official bio says, "As an award-winning author, poet, speaker, and artist, Brent Sampson understands the mania of the muse and how to infuse success into every creative endeavor. Brent's proficiencies with selling, marketing, publishing, and coaching inspired him to launch Outskirts Press in 2002, one of the fastest growing on-demand publishing companies in America."

I've poked fun at some of the stupid mistakes in his books and on his company's website.

Brent has recently issued the second edition of *Self-Publishing Simplified*. He apparently realized that I was right and he was wrong about "offset" vs. "off-set" printing. He even followed my advice and changed his foreword into an introduction. In the introduction, he fixed one really stupid error which I pointed out, where he had the wrong name for the author of *Roget's Thesaurus*.

However, he did not fix the BS about the "headaches" from getting an ISBN and bar code, and "paying thousands of dollars to print thousands of books."

In 2007 Brent distributed a list of "Top 5 Shenanigans of 5 Print-on-Demand Publishers" to point out the failings of his competitors. He mentions such things as phony offers to publish for free, and loss of author's rights.

Since Brent does not list his own company's BS-ing, I'm glad to do it for him.

Perhaps his most outrageous fiction is this: "The majority of independently self-published authors find it nearly impossible to secure distribution through book wholesalers like Ingram and Baker & Taylor."

First of all, unless Brent is capable of large-scale mind-reading, he has *no way of knowing* the experiences of the majority of any kind of people.

Second — and more important — it just isn't true.

If a self-publishing author has books printed on demand by Lightning Source (the leading POD printer for both independents like me and companies like Brent's), there are NO unsold copies for the author to deal with, and it is *far from impossible* to secure distribution through Ingram and Baker & Taylor.

In fact, it's almost impossible NOT to do it, because it happens automatically. All an author has to do is approve a proof for printing, and the rest just happens.

At the end of this chapter you'll see a long list of some of the booksellers offering one of my independently self-pubbed books, *I Only Flunk My Brightest Students: stories from school and real life.*

I was amazed at the number of sellers. It was, of course, important and nice for the book to be offered by Amazon and B&N. I didn't even know that Target sold books but they're trying to sell four of mine now. Target will even accept book returns, but I never have to issue a refund.

I never heard of some of the booksellers.

Some of them — like FarsiDictionary.com — seem ridiculous.

My book cover proclaims "Dirty Parts Easy To Find," but it has been offered on a children's book website! I was amazed to find three companies that want to RENT my book.

But the most amazing thing is that I did ABSO-LUTELY NOTHING to get any of these 30-plus companies to offer my book.

Brent **S**ampson has the perfect initials.

Ignorant or dishonest?

As the head of a publishing company, and someone who brags about his proficiency in publishing, Brent has a lot to learn about the publishing business.

Of course, maybe he really *does* know the truth, but doesn't want others to know it. People who do know the truth may not want to do business with him.

Brent's website warns of the "hassles of independent self-publishing, like guessing print-runs, managing inventory, and the responsibility of order fulfillment."

Well, I'm an independent self-publisher, and I *never ever* think about print runs, inventory or order fulfillment. Actually, the biggest hassles I deal with are typos.

Brent says independent self-publishers "are left with thousands of unsold copies and without an effective way of getting their books into the hands of readers" and "The independently self published authors I know all have boxes of books in their garage and park their cars on the street."

Apparently Brent knows the wrong people. He certainly doesn't know me.

Brent also wrote about the high costs of setting up websites. That's baloney intended to make his own company look good. Actually, it costs very little to set up a website, and it can be done without Brent's assistance.

Rent Brent's brain

If you trust Brent Sampson's knowledge and opinions, he'll be glad to give you personal advice on the phone — for $250 per hour.

He's also available for hire as a public speaker. He lists "Independent self-publishing vs. print-on-demand. What's the difference?" as one of his topics. I'd love to hear him try to explain that (but I wouldn't *pay* to hear it).

I'm an independent self-publisher *and* I use print-on-demand.

Independent self-publishing and POD are *not* incompatible or opposites. They often go together.

Brent's stupid topic is like asking, "What's the difference between farming and a tractor?" They often go together. Brent wants to charge money to answer a question that does not have to be asked.

And a personal memo to Brent: Not only were you wrong about "off-set" vs. "offset," you're also wrong about "to whit." The correct phrase is "to wit." And in your bio, the final phrase "one of the fastest growing on-demand publishing companies in America" should come after "Outskirts Press," not after "2002." Also, you should kill

24

the commas between "speaker" and "artist" and between "publishing" and "and coaching." Aren't you supposed to *be* a writing coach? Didn't you major in English in college? And while you're at it, fix the misspelled "importantly" on your website.

Even publishers need editors. If Brent used one of the Outskirts Press editors, either the editor is unsuited to the job, or is afraid to correct the boss. Maybe both.

How difficult is it?

Brent Sampson claims to be a "publishing expert." He insists that it's extremely difficult for independently self-published authors to get their books distributed. It's not.

Here are just some of the companies selling my books — with absolutely NO effort by me:

Amazon	Alibris	Amazon (Germany)
Barnes & Noble	StyleFeeder	Webster (Italy)
Abebooks	Amazon Canada	Alpha Music (Germany)
Page 1 Book	eCampus.com	Booklooker (Germany)
Better World	Biblio	Bol.ch (Switzerland)
A1Books	Powells	Libri.de (Germany)
Target	Papa Media	Amazon (Japan)
Books A Million	FarsiDictionary.com	Sumonto.com
TextbooksRus	Amazon (UK)	Chegg Rentals
TextbookX	Buch.de (Germany)	Campus Book Rentals
Discount Book Sale	Alibris (UK)	BookRenter.com
FlipKart (India)	Abebooks (UK)	Rediff Books (India)

From Yahoo Answers:

I have had nothing but troubles and delay since last February in getting my children's storybook published by Outskirts Press. They have changed representatives on me three times and there is no coordination between them so each time it's like starting over. The colorizers were terrible so I finally decided to use the colored images I sent in instead which they are "cleaning" up but which I am still having to pay the colorization fee for. And it seems that they have been just sitting on it and that nothing has been done. They tell me that they are finally sending the images for proofing tomorrow but I'm not counting on it. ... I'm really beginning to think they are bogus and just taking my money which was close to $3,000.00.

Chapter 4 (4/16/09)
More Picking on Outskirts Press

A few readers have complained that I "pick on" Outskirts Press. I don't think that I'm really picking on them, but they do so many things wrong, they invite criticism.

Outskirts seems uncertain and insecure about the nature of its business. The company has previously said it provided "custom book publishing," and "on-demand publishing," but in the latest version of its puff book, it self-applies a new label: "Independent Self-Printing." Maybe next year it will be apple coring or car washing or dog walking or going-out-of-business.

Yesterday, customer service guy Karl Schroeder sent me a "happy anniversary" email (which coincidentally arrived on my birthday). Karl reminded me that yesterday was a year since he first started trying to seduce me.

Karl wrote, "Believe it or not, it has been 1 year to the day that we first started emailing you about publishing with Outskirts Press. Hopefully our emails over the months have been helpful to you. I know the publishing journey isn't always an easy one. There are many decisions to be made, and sometimes the choices are confusing."

Despite the usual sloppy writing ("1" instead of "one" and overused clichés) the email made me realize that the more I know about Outskirts, the more reasons I have to stay away from them, and to urge others to do the same.

Avoiding Karl's company was certainly not a "confusing" choice. His emails have been very "helpful" — in convincing me to avoid Outskirts.

Karl claims that one Outskirts author, "Instead of $3.74 per book, he started making nearly $14 for every book he sold on Amazon."

Instead of using Outskirts, I formed my own publishing company which uses the same POD printer that Outskirts does. On one of my books sold by Amazon, I collect $18.38 per copy.

Almost any writer can do it, too.

A challenge to Outskirts Press: prove you're not full of crap

A few days ago Outskirts Press rep Karl Schroeder sent me an email saying, "Many authors have discovered that switching to Outskirts Press is more profitable for them... For one recent best-selling author on Amazon, switching to Outskirts Press from 'Publisher A' was the best decision he ever made. His royalties increased from 15% of his retail price to 55% of his retail price as a result. Instead of $3.74 per book, he started making nearly $14 for every book he sold on Amazon."

Using some basic junior high school math, Karl's numbers point to a cover price for the book of $24.95. Karl claims that the author is getting nearly $14 (likely $13.72). HOWEVER, if you use the royalty tables on the Outskirts website, the numbers are VERY DIFFERENT.

A 400 page paperback book with a $24.95 price pays royalties of $1.12, $2.12 or $3.12, depending on the publishing package the author decides to buy from Outskirts.

A 300 page book with a $24.95 price pays royalties of $2.72, $3.72 or $4.72.

A 200 page book with a $24.95 price (a bit of a stretch for a 200-page book) pays $4.32, $5.32 or $6.32.

6 X 9 common

	Diamond	Ruby	Sapphire
6 x 9 Paperback cream			
Enter your book's **ESTIMATED** page count at publication:	**45**		
Three - Customize Your Pricing		(Pricing uses page ‹ printed book of	
Use the "Click to Increase Price" button for more package choice			
Retail Price	$24.95	$24.95	$24.95
Royalty	$7.96	$6.96	$5.96
Author Discount	81%	77%	73%
+ CLICK TO INCREASE PRICING +		- CLICK TO DECREASE PRICING -	

A puny 45 page book (minimum possible size) with an absurd $24.95 price pays $5.96, $6.96 or $7.96.

Even if I decreased the page size from the common 6×9-inch size to a smaller 5×8 size to save bit of paper, the royalties did not increase.

If I "force" the online royalty calculator to work out the numbers for a 300-page "deluxe" hard-cover jacketed book with a $24.95 price, the royalties are NEGATIVE $1.93, $2.93 or $4.93!

➔ **It looks like the only way that Outskirts could pay a 55% royalty on a $24.95 book would be if the book had *no pages*. I doubt that many people would pay $24.95 for an empty cover.**

OK, Karl or Brent, I'd like to see your numbers. I invite you to prove me wrong.

$30,000 book royalties in one month? It's time to pick on Outskirts Press again.

Outskirts Press and its often-clueless boss Brent Sampson have been my frequent targets.

I don't hate them. I'm glad they exist because they give me something to write about. They are easy and amusing targets because they combine ignorance, incompetence and sleaziness, with great visibility.

Outskirts Press is a vanity publisher, a company that makes most of its money by selling services to writers, not by selling books to readers.

Outskirts has previously called its business "custom book publishing" and "on-demand publishing," but has recently adopted a new label: "Independent Self-Printing." They're trying to capture some glamour and credibility from "indie" musicians and film makers.

The company uses scare tactics in an effort to capture business from would-be *real* indie publishers. Outskirts lies about the alleged difficulties of getting an ISBN bar code and selling books online.

It warns of the "hassles of independent self-publishing, like guessing print-runs, managing inventory, and the responsibility of order fulfillment." I'm an inde-

31

pendent self-publisher, and I *never ever* think about print runs, inventory or order fulfillment.

One recent publicity outburst from Outskirts has highlighted their customer/author Gang Chen, who "has earned over $100,000 in author royalties in six short months."

Chen wrote on a blog that "In one month (January 2009), I earned over $30,000 in Royalties ($31,207.68, to be precise). I earned even more in February."

Outskirts says Chen "will receive a first-quarter royalty check in the amount of $77,611.88 for books sold between [sic] January-March 2009. This follows a previous royalty check of $33,679.56 that Chen recently received from Outskirts Press for books sold between [sic] October-December 2008."

Chen's blog offers some useful advice, but don't be fooled by the headline, "**How You Can Earn $30,000 a Month through POD Publishing.**"

Chen's experience is *extremely atypical* and no one should salivate while dreaming of emulating him. Be aware of three things:

(1) Chen's book is *highly specialized*. It's a study guide needed for professional advancement. It's a very important book aimed at a very small audience for whom the book price is not significant. It's like a college textbook that students must buy for $150 in order to take a course needed for graduation.

(2) Because of the *small audience*, it's highly unlikely that the sales volume (about 1,000 copies per month) and royalty payments will stay at the recent high level month-after-month, year-after-year.

(3) Despite its small page size and mere 243 pages, it has a *huge cover price* of **$69.95**. Amazon discounts it by just 10% to $62.95.

I compliment Chen for filling a need and getting paid well for it. HOWEVER, if he became a *real, independent self-publisher* instead of using Outskirts, he probably could have made *even more money*.

Use the "Click to Increase Price" butto		
		Diamond
Retail Price		$69.95
Royalty		$28.18
Author Discount		90%
+ CLICK TO INCREASE PRICING +		-

According to the Outskirts chart (above), if Chen paid $999 or more for an Outskirts "Diamond" package, he earns $28.18 per book.

If, on the other hand, Chen decided to do a little bit more work himself, or hired a freelance designer and editor possibly for less than what he paid to Outskirts, he could have had the books produced directly by Lightning Source (the same printer that Outskirts often uses) for just $4.54 per book plus a small set-up fee.

◆With Outskirts Press as the publisher, each $69.95-list book earns $28.18 for author Gang Chen.

◆If Chen self-published and kept the $69.95 list price, he could have made $51.42 per book — nearly twice what Outskirts pays him!

◆Alternatively, if Chen is satisfied with $28.18 per book, by self-publishing he could have reduced the list price of the book to just $40.95, instead of $69.95. He could sell more books and make more money.

◆By using Outskirts Press, Gang Chen is making less money than he could be making, or his readers are paying more for his books than they could be paying — or both.

**With Outskirts Press,
a $69.95 book earns $28.18.**

**With self-publishing,
a $69.95 book earns $51.42,
or a $40.95 book earns $28.18.**

Chapter 7 (8/15/09)
More lies from Outskirts Press

Outskirts Press wants prospective author/customers to think they are a "self-publishing company," but they're not. (More about that later.)

The company recently distributed some alleged "news" via several of the freebie press release services (not the first-class services that charge for distributing releases and get better pickup by the news media).

In addition to suffering from limited media impact, freebie PR services also display ads from competitors.

The page at PR.com with the Outskirts news release has bold, colorful ads promoting the publishing services of Tate Publishing and Booksurge with clickable links to take readers right to the Tate and Booksurge websites.

It takes two clicks to go from the Outskirts press release page to the Outskirts website — but of course the competitors paid money and Outskirts went the cheap route.

The headline writer wants the world to know that *Inc* magazine declared Outskirts to be the "Fastest-Growing Self Publishing Company."

Forget, for a moment, that Outskirts is not a self-publishing company.

The release stupidly says: "sales of self-publishing books climbed 132% while the sales of traditionally published books fell by 3%."

"Self-publishing books" would be books *about* self-publishing. I think someone at Outskirts meant "self-published" books.

Even worse, Outskirts is seriously distorting the statistics (originally provided by R. R. Bowker). The 132% growth was for *on-demand books*, which include *much* more than self-published books. Major traditional publishing companies now print-on-demand, as do university presses, vanity presses, and real self-publishers.

(Here's the actual statement from Bowker: "Bowker projects that 285,394 On Demand books were produced last year, a staggering 132% increase over last year's final total of 123,276 titles.")

And, of course, authors who use companies like Outskirts are not really self-publishing.

If Outskirts is the publisher, the author is *not* the publisher; and you can't be a self-publisher if you are not a publisher. Just as no one can take a bath for you or take medicine for you, no one can self-publish for you.

Outskirts is notorious for deception, exaggeration, and stupid errors. Company boss Brent Sampson wrote a book that apparently had no editor or a blind editor. Or maybe none of his employees would dare correct the boss. His key employees are relatives.

Brent promotes himself as a "best-selling author." I've twice asked for some specifics about his bestseller status, but never received an answer.

A book about flea removal from pregnant three-legged albino Weimaraners could sell exactly one copy and still be the BESTSELLER in its field. There is no law that requires an explanation for a bestseller claim. Anyone can call any book is a bestseller.

The press release says that from 2005 through 2008, "Outskirts Press grew at a rate of 850.5%, making it the fastest growing self-publishing and book marketing company and #268 among all American businesses. Outskirts Press is the 21st fastest-growing business in the Consumer Products & Services category."

Even the last sentence is misleading. Book publishing is certainly not a *consumer* service. If Outskirts was more properly listed in *Business* Products and Services, its ranking would drop a few places.

In truth, Outskirts Press might be #268 among the businesses that submitted information to *Inc* magazine, or among the businesses that the magazine analyzed. But only the IRS has the statistics to judge business growth. And companies can lie to both the IRS and Inc.

Additionally, *Inc's* rankings are of "America's Fastest-Growing *Private* Companies" — not ALL American companies, as Outskirts wants us to believe.

And, of course, *Inc* ranks only those companies that submitted data to the magazine. Many successful private companies prefer secrecy to publicity.

Inc conveniently supplies a press release template for use by honorees.

Here's part of it: "*Inc* magazine today ranked COMPANY NAME NO. XX on its 28th annual Inc. 500, an exclusive ranking of the nation's fastest-growing private companies."

Here's how Outskirts modified the template to remove the reference to "private companies": "Inc Magazine released their annual Inc 500 list of the nation's fastest-growing businesses."

Look at the headline in the Outskirts press release: "*Inc* 500 Names Outskirts Press Fastest-Growing Self Publishing Company."

In truth, *Inc never* applied that description to Outskirts Press.

Outskirts Press is a vanity press that calls itself a "self-publishing company."

It grows by exploiting ignorance and gullibility. As journalists and prospective customers continue to catch the company's lies, distortions and stupid errors, its growth will *not* continue.

The Outskirts company profile published by *Inc* says that the company's 2008 sales were $4.6 million. While that revenue is equal to three or four McDonald's restaurants, it does *not* mean the company is a titan in the publishing business.

Business information service provider Manta.com said that Outskirts competitor Author Solutions "has an annual revenue of $29,300,000 and employs a staff of approximately 260."

Random House, the world's largest English-language general trade book publisher, reportedly has annual sales of about $2.3 billion and about 6,000 employees.

Outskirts Press has a long way to go.

No. 268

Outskirts Press

Parker, CO

Year	2009
Industry	Consumer Products & Services
Founded	2002
Growth	850.5%
2005 Revenue	$480,482
2008 Revenue	$4.6 million
Employees	3

Above, the Outskirts Press company profile published by *Inc* says that Outskirts has *just three employees*. Judging by the poor quality of the company's output, those three people must be terribly
overworked, or uneducated, or stupid.

B.S. from <u>B</u>rent <u>Sa</u>mpson

(Don't believe any of this.)

"Excessive print-runs are only part of the problem. The majority of independently self-published authors find it nearly impossible to secure distribution through book wholesalers like Ingram and Baker & Taylor. As a result, they are left with thousands of unsold copies and without an effective way of getting their books into the hands of readers."

Truth from Brent Sampson

"Writing a bad book is easier than writing a good one. "

(Brent has lots of experience with bad books.)

Chapter 8 (8/19/09)
More incompetence from Outskirts Press

Outskirts Press does such a lousy job promoting its own business in press releases and promotional books that I would not expect the company to be much help to their author/customers, either.

For $99, they'll send out a "standard press release" to announce a new book. Customers can also buy a "custom press release" for $199.

The Outskirts press releases that I've seen, prepared both for Outskirts and for it author/customers, are amateurish and error-filled. Additionally, rather than use the paid-for press release distribution services that get more respect from the news media, Outskirts uses freebie services that are usually ignored by the media, or that don't distribute releases to the right media.

Fresno, CA, August 12, 2009 --(PR.com)-- Outskirts Press, Inc. has published Diamond by Alan Robertson, which is the author's most recent book to date. The 5 x 8 Paperback cream in the Fiction category is available worldwide on book retailer websites such as Amazon and Barnes & Noble for a suggested retail price of $9.95. The webpage at www.outskirtspress.com/alanrobertson2 was launched simultaneously with the book's publication.

A Google search for a key phrase in the release I show on the previous page for *Diamond* shows exactly FOUR links. Three links go to the free PR services, and one link is for a British blog. That's pathetic, and *not* the way to sell books.

A similar search for a key phrase from the Outskirts book *Eternal Life* (chosen at random from the list of recent releases above) also shows exactly four Google links — and each one is for a PR distribution website!

Apparently *not even one* other website thought it was newsworthy. Outskirts does not know how to sell books, but they do know how to collect money from ignorant authors.

By comparison, a news release for one of my books, distributed through PRWeb (which is not a freebie), was picked up by hundreds of websites. Even many months later, it is still on about 90 sites.

The fragment of a custom press release on the previous page shows the abysmal quality of Outskirts' release writing. It has bad grammar, extraneous words, improper typography, ugly justification, non-sentences, etc. The release is not worth $1.99, let alone $199.

If you look at the group of Google links for Outskirts books, you'll see that three different books are *all* described as "deftly constructed at 215 pages...."

I don't know if all of the books were constructed with equal deftness, but it's obvious that the actual releases are not particularly deft. *Daft* might be a better adjective.

I find it strange that the three randomly selected books all have the same number of pages. It's also strange that they have 215 pages. Since a piece of paper has TWO sides, a page count is almost always shown as an even number, whether or not the number includes blank pages at the back of a book.

In addition to the "deftly constructed phrase" that seems to appear in every Outskirts press release, the company uses the similarly ubiquitous "being aggressively promoted to appropriate markets."

If the press releases are ignored by the media, Outskirts has a lot to learn about aggressive promotion.

It appears that Outskirts Press is run by a bunch of ignorant fools. Sadly, its customers seem to be equally deficient.

From the Outskirts author contract:

"Outskirts Press's total liability to Author or any third-party for any and all damages shall not exceed in the aggregate the amount of fees actually paid by Author to Outskirts Press during the one month period prior to Outskirts Press' act giving rise to the liability."

If the author paid $5,000 two months before the screw-up, but didn't pay anything in the immediately preceding month, the author gets nothing — even if the Outskirts error costs the author a million bucks.

Chapter 9 (12/7/09)
Outskirts Press keeps getting stupider

Outskirts Press is a frequent subject of my wrath and ridicule because the company does so many things so badly, and boss Brent Sampson is careless, ignorant and dishonest.

The latest Outskirts offense is a silly email blast sent to potential customers from Karl, Elizabeth and Chris in their Author Services department.

This is the first paragraph:

>>I hope you're having a good day so far. I'd like to tell you a little about our Marketing COACH. In fact, below you will find an example of the type of emailed marketing information and promotion advice that is included with our Diamond and Pearl books after publication. Consider it a taste to whet your appetite to publish with Outskirts Press. You can meet your author representative in your author's center by clicking on the GET YOUR AUTHOR REP button when you are ready at http://outskirtspres.com/authors.php<<

Unfortunately, that linked website is NOT for Outskirts Press, because the three geniuses omitted the final "s" in "outskirtspress." The error was not caught by the

45

"dedicated group of publishing professionals" at Outskirts who also missed boss Brent's many errors.

Instead of taking readers to the Outskirts Press website, the erroneous link goes to a site operated by a "URL poacher" which makes money because of mistyped web addresses.

So, we have a carelessly crafted promotional email sent out by Outskirts Press, in an effort to impress people about Outskirts' promotional abilities, that delivers potential Outskirts customers to Outskirts' competitors!

Also: the first word in the email is "I," but the email is signed by three people. This is the kind of silly incompetence I've come to expect from Outskirts.

I hope no one would trust them to publish a book. On the other hand, I don't want the company to go out of business, because the Outskirts idiots give me so much to write about.

Chapter 10 (12/16/09)
Stupid and cheap Outskirts Press helps competitors

Above, Outskirts Press's press releases often carry advertising for its competitors. Outskirts doesn't pay for the press releases, but its competitors pay for the ads.

Outskirts Press is the vanity press I love to hate. I urge writers to stay away from Outskirts because its people are inept and dishonest, but those same characteristics give me lots to write about.

Outskirts management and staff are like *The Gang That Couldn't Shoot Straight*.

- When they try to draw guns, they shoot themselves in the feet.
- When they try to instruct and advise, they reveal how little they know.
- When they try to be competitive, they create opportunities for their competitors.

Outskirts frequently sends out press releases promoting their author-customers, and tooting their own horn.

Rather than spend money with first-class news distribution services like PR Web, PR Newswire or Business Wire, Outskirts instead does it the cheap way, with no-cost news services like PR Log, PR.com, Newswire Today and Free-Press-Release.com.

The freebie services generally get little attention from media. When I checked, I saw that a release for an Outskirts book, *Eternal Life*, was not picked up by even one website.

The services that Outskirts uses often present **ADS FOR COMPETITORS** of Outskirts — on the same web page!

Was Outskirts too lazy to check, too blind to see, or too stupid to care?

On the previous page you can see some alleged news about Outskirts that was distributed at no charge by PR Log. Since Outskirts doesn't pay PR Log, PR Log must get income from somewhere. They carry pay-per-click ads which target key words in the press releases.

So, the Outskirts news that is intended to get customers for Outskirts, runs right alongside vanity press ads for Tate, Trafford, CreateSpace, Lulu, iUniverse, Dorrance, AuthorHouse and perhaps others. Those companies are paying money to take potential customers away from Outskirts, which was unwilling to pay a few hundred bucks for news distribution free of promos for its competitors.

Outskirts Press is cheap, stupid, ignorant, deceptive and self-defeating.

It's OK to use the company for laughs, but not for publishing.

> "Errors in your writing cause readers to question your credibility."
>
> –Brent Sampson, founder & CEO of Outskirts Press

Outskirts Press idiots show how NOT to write a press release

Outskirts Press announces Romancing A Mystery from Burbank, IL author Evelyn Cullet.

[Unless the author is J. D. Salinger or J. K. Rowling, the mere publication of a book is NOT news. Is there anything in that headline that offers a reason to buy the book? Does anyone care who is making the announcement? Does anyone care that the author comes from Burbank, Illinois? Does anyone know why the letter "A" in the book title is in upper case? The book title should have been in italics, or in quotes, to separate it from the rest of the text.]

Outskirts Press, Inc. [Who cares if the business was incorporated?] has published Romancing A [Should not be upper case.] Mystery by Evelyn Cullet, which is the author's most recent book to date. [If it's her most recent book, there is no reason to say "to date." Actually, it may be her only book.] The 5 x 8 Paperback [Paperback should not be in upper case.] cream [What the hell is a "Paperback cream?" I suppose it's less fattening than ice cream. Oh, I see:

51

cream is the color of the paper the book is printed on. Will anyone make a buying decision based on paper color? If the paper color really *is* important, the sentence should have been written better.] in the FICTION / General category [FICTION does not have to be in upper case, nor does the "G" in "General," and the category is unlikely a reason to buy. We already have a pretty good indication that the book is fiction.] is available worldwide [Yeah, just like almost every other book in the world.] on book retailer websites such as Amazon and Barnes & Noble [Yeah, just like almost every other book in the world.] for a suggested retail price of $19.95. The webpage [Most people spell "web page" as two words, but I'll let it go since I write "website" — but I really don't like the "bp" combination.] at www.outskirtspress.com/romancingamystery was launched simultaneously with the book's publication. [Oh goody, the author has a web page. That means this must be a good book and I'll have to buy it.]

Meet Charlotte Ross. [I guess the author likes *charlotte russe* cake.] A young woman in her prime, [A young woman *should* be in her prime. If she was young and *past* her prime, *then* it would be worth mentioning.] she's become bored living in the small Illinois town [Gee, the author is also from a small Illinois town. How inventive — NOT! And how irrelevant. Who cares where the small town is?] where she grew up and is tired of her mom [I'm tired of finding the childlike "mom" in serious writing and broadcasting. Let's go back to "mother" except for quotations.] trying to marry her off to the oldest and wealthiest men in town. [If this was a TV show, at this point I'd switch to **CNBC or Animal Planet.]** So when her mystery-loving friend Jane Marshall **[That name deserves an award for blandness. Why not another name derived from a cake? She could be Banana Cream or Deborah Devilsfood.]** suggests a driving trip across England and Ireland, Charlotte eagerly packs her bags. **[A silly outdated cliche — they're probably suitcases, not bags.]** But Charlotte is about to get more than she bargained for. Just two days in, **[In what?]** their car breaks down and the women take refuge inside Blake Hall **[Ooh-ooh. I bet it has ghosts.]**, an ancient aristocrat's lair **[Sounds like the BatCave.]** with a long and rumored past. **[That goes well with "a dark and stormy night."]** As guests of the handsome **[Well, if he's handsome, I'll definitely buy the book.]** Lord Peter Montigue **[Montague would have been a better choice. It was the last name of Romeo, Juliet Capulet's boyfriend.]** Blake, the girls **[Girls? We were first told that Charlotte is a "young woman," and then that they were both "women."]** waste little time getting into plenty of trouble: ruining a priceless painting, encountering alleged **ghosts [AHA! I was right about the ghosts. But who alleged that they were ghosts, and why can't we have some *real* ones in the book?]** and stumbling upon a gruesome corpse **[As opposed to a really pleasant corpse.]**. The latter **["Latter" is OK for a contract, but not a press release.]** will draw them into a centuries-old mystery that has remained unsolved, until now at least. **[If it's unsolved, it's unsolved until now at least.]** Through it all, these out-of-place Americans also find the last thing they'd ever imagined: unexpected romance. **[Chances are, as young women on a road trip, they *did* imagine find-**

53

ing romance, and it's probably *not* the last thing they imagined. Finding Queen Elizabeth wandering drunk and naked on the road might be the last thing they'd imagine. And who is the romance with? With ghosts? With the handsome lord? With each other?] Smart, savvy [People can be smart and savvy, but can a book be that way?] and at times uproariously funny [I hope it's as funny as the press release.], Romancing a [Oh good, for a change we get a lower case "a."] Mystery is part Jane Austen, part Agatha Christie and part Sir Arthur Conan Doyle with just a touch of Oscar Wilde thrown in to spice things up [Oscar was apparently gay, so being thrown in somewhere with Sir Arthur could have been spicy, but Oscar probably wouldn't care about Jane and Agatha.] for an unforgettable story that's all its own. [What does "all its own" mean, or add? If I buy the book, will it be "all *my* own?"]

Deftly constructed at 352 pages, [EVERY damn book published by Outskirts is said to be "deftly constucted." Another Outskirts book is "Deftly constructed at 52 pages." Perhaps it's much defter than this one is.] Romancing A [Should be lower case.] Mystery is being aggressively promoted to appropriate markets ["aggressively promoted" is another phrase that appears in every press release for an Outskirts Press book. It means that Outskirts is using freebie press release distribution services to send out news that will likely be ignored.] with a focus on the FICTION / General category. [If we didn't care about the category the first time, we still don't care about it the second time, and we still don't like the upper casing.] With U.S. wholesale distribution through Ingram and Baker & Taylor, **[That may impress the author, but it means nothing to readers.]** and pervasive online availability **[That's a phrase we don't often encounter — except in about 130,000 other online items about Outskirts books.]** through Amazon, Barnes & Noble and elsewhere, Romancing A **[Should be lower case.]** Mystery meets consumer demand **[Which consumers have demanded it?]** through both retail and library markets with a suggested retail price of $19.95. **[That's a very high price.]**

Additionally, Romancing A **[Should be lower case]** Mystery can be ordered by retailers or wholesalers for the maximum trade discount price set by the author **[Who the hell cares who sets the price; and wouldn't retailers and wholesalers want to buy at the MINIMUM price, not the maximum price? Buyers want the maximum discount, but the minimum price.]** in quantities of ten **[Should be "10."]** or more from the Outskirts Press wholesale online bookstore at www.outskirtspress.com/buybooks

ISBN: 9781432746667 Format: 5 x 8 Paperback cream SRP: $19.95 **[Yeah, yeah. We know that already. "Paperback" should be lower case, and it would be nice to have some punctuation or a line break after the ISBN and "cream." Actually, this stuff really belongs on a "sell sheet," not in a press release aimed at the general public.]**

About the Author

Evelyn Cullet is a longtime mystery buff. A former member of the Agatha Christie Society **[Did Agatha throw her out?]**, she is a current member of Sisters In Crime

[The release could have said that she "has been a member" of both organizations, without revealing that she is no longer a member of the Christie Club.], the worldwide organization for women mystery writers. Now retired from the offices [How many offices did she retire from, and didn't she really retire from the company, not from the offices? That phrase reminds me of the stupid notepads that say "from the desk of..."] of a major soft drink company, she spends part of her time organic gardening [Are her experiences with compost and sugary fizzy water reasons to buy the book?], and the rest doing what she loves best: writing. [Hmm. She spends part of her time gardening and the rest of her time writing. That leaves no time for eating, bathing, sleeping, shopping, socializing, anything. Evelyn doesn't seem to have much of a life — unless the press release writer made a MISTAKE. Is that possible?]

About Outskirts Press, Inc. [Nobody cares about the "Inc."]

Outskirts Press, Inc. [Nobody cares about the "Inc."] offers full-service, custom self-publishing [Actually, they don't offer any kind of self-publishing. No company or person can self-publish for anyone else.] and book marketing services for authors seeking a cost-effective, fast, and flexible [What do they mean by that?] way to publish and distribute their books worldwide while retaining all their rights and full creative control. [Not if the design and editing are done by Outskirts people.] Available for authors globally [Damn. Apparently the writers on Neptune will have to find another publisher.] at www.outskirtspress.com

and located on the outskirts of Denver, Colorado [Outskirts is on the outskirts. How cute. Is the location of the publisher's office a reason to buy the book? Are we supposed to be so excited from reading the press release that we'll drive to Colorado to buy a book?], Outskirts Press represents the future of book publishing [Uh-oh. We're in deep shit, folks.] , today.

The press release contact is Kelly Schuknecht. Kelly is "Director of Author Support" at Outskirts, and was previously their "Press Release Coordinator." We can't be absolutely sure that she wrote this crap, but she certainly had the opportunity to read it and fix it. Kelly has a degree in Modern Foreign Languages from James Madison University. It's too bad she doesn't have a degree in ENGLISH!

On the other hand, Jeanine Sampson, Outskirts COO and wife of Outskirts boss Brent Sampson, apparently *does* have a degree in English from the Univ. of Virginia. Maybe she could help. OOPS! Forget about it. I just saw a press release sent out over Jeanine's name last year. It has the same goofy "most recent book to date," "Deftly constructed at," "maximum trade discount price" and "pervasive online availability" phrases that Kelly uses.

Message to the author: I have not read your book. It may be superb, and it sounds like a lot of fun, but I don't like your inept publisher. Maybe this publicity will help you sell some books. Good luck. I hope you write better than the person who wrote your press release

A publisher should know better

Brent Sampson's book, *Self-Publishing Simplified,* has a foreword written by Brent — which goes against the normal book-publishing rules that any publisher *should* know. Forewords are not supposed to be written by the author! Brent should have called it a "preface" or an "introduction" or hired someone else to write a foreword.

An Outskirts victim speaks: Outskirts Press editing is like "no editing at all."

I have frequently preached about the necessity of paying for professional editing of self-published and pay-to-publish books.

Unfortunately, there is no licensing exam or certification process required before someone is allowed to use the "editor" label. People tend to trust the editorial staffs at publishers, and may end up paying a lot of money for inferior editing which can severely damage a book that has been lovingly labored over for years.

Outskirts Press apparently has some terrible editors. Even a book written by Outskirts Press boss Brent Sampson is filled with stupid errors that no legitimate editor would have ignored.

What follows is a slightly modified email from an Outskirts author/customer/victim. This author paid $999 for the most expensive "Diamond" publishing package, plus extra-cost options including nearly $1,000 for "professional" editing.

I wish I would have read your blog before I published my first novel with Outskirts. I have had some scathing reviews due to the errors that were left in my book after I paid a small fortune for editing with the Outskirts editing team.

I was so excited when my book was first released, but after a few family members pointed out the mistakes left behind, I can't describe the restraint it took for me not to explode.

I tried to reason with my so-called marketing representative, but she simply hid behind the "fine print" they give you *after* they receive payment from you. It would have cost me another small fortune to revise the book, and I am still in debt from publishing it in the first place. The marketing representative simply would not assume any responsibility for mistakes that Outskirts made.

Outskirts made me feel paranoid about not getting their editing service, but when I did it was as if I had no editing at all. The only consolation that I have, is that I have a few fans that were willing to give me a chance as a new author. They loved my book.

I'm sure other writers would hate to be scammed out of their money for a service as unreliable as Outskirts' editing. I purchased the editing service for peace of mind, not to hold my breath each time a review comes out, only to be criticized for editing I paid for but did not receive.

This suggests another advantage of being a "real" self-publisher instead of using a company like Outskirts Press. Despite extensive checking and professional editing, I've found about six typos in one of my books. The total cost for me to make the changes, including getting a proof shipped for next-day delivery from my printer, was just $30.

NO SURPRISE: The Outskirts Press contract avoids responsibility for errors and has a stupid typo.
BIG SURPRISE: authors might loan Outskirts money for six months, interest-free!

Here are some highlights from the Outskirts Press author contract, with my comments in bold:

Author receives 100% of the royalties profit for each wholesale print copy sold for which Outskirts Press receives payment. **[If you work your ass off promoting your book, and pay Outskirts to promote your book, but Outskirts sells copies of your book and doesn't get paid, you don't get paid.]**

Royalties are paid to Author within 90 days following the end of the calendar quarter in which Wholesale Book Sales occurred **[If a book is sold on January 1, Outskirts doesn't have to pay you your royalties until 90 days starting on April 1 (i.e., the end of June — six months later!).**

The Outskirts Press online bookstore offers discounts of up to 55% on purchases of 10 or more books to "Wholesalers, retailers, distributors," and requires payment by credit card. A bookseller's money should be in the Outskirts checking account two days after a purchase, but Outskirts doesn't have to pay you until up to 178 days later.

You will become Outskirts' bank, potentially loaning it money for nearly half a year, but not being paid any interest.

Outskirts will cancel your book if you don't pay their $25 annual digital storage and hosting fee within 30 days, but you must allow them six months to pay you. Conceivably, your book could be canceled if you owe them $25 for 31 days, even while they owe you hundreds or thousands of dollars.]

Outskirts Press does not warrant that the service or product provided will be uninterrupted or error free. [That's certainly no surprise.] Outskirts Press disclaims any and all representations and warranties, expressed or implied, including, without limitation, the implied warranties of merchantability, salability, or non-infringement of copyright. [In other words, don't expect Outskirts to do anything right.]

Outskirts Press's total liability to Author or any third-party for any and all damages shall not exceed in the aggregate the amount of fees actually paid by Author to Outskirts Press during the one month period prior to Outskirts Press' act giving rise to the liability. [If the author paid $5,000 two months before the screw-up, but didn't pay anything in the immediately preceding month, the author gets nothing -- even if the Outskirts error costs the author a million bucks.]

To the maximum extent permitted by applicable law, in no event shall Outskirts Press, its parent companies, subsidiaries, or affiliates, or any of their respective officers, directors, employees, or agents by **[TYPO: should be "be."]** liable for punitive, consequential, incidental, exemplary, indirect, or special damages, including without limitation damages for loss of profits, revenues, business data, or other intangibles, whether or not such damages were foreseeable and even if Outskirts Press had been advised of the possibility or likelihood of such damages. **[In other words, if Outskirts Press screws up, don't expect them to pay for any loss caused by their errors — even if they knew in advance about the problem.]**

Any legal action related to the terms of or obligations arising under this Agreement shall be brought in the District Court of Douglas County, State of Colorado. **[If you live in Hawaii or New Hampshire, and you don't like what Outskirts did to your book, you have to travel to Castle Rock, Colorado to sue them.]**

Outskirts says its mission statement is "To exceed the expectations of every author we help publish."

In reality, authors can expect crappy books and inadequate promotion from a company that hides behind legal weaseling, denies any obligation to do the right thing, and may deny any liability when they do the wrong thing.

Selling what doesn't exist (part 1)

Outskirts Press — like many vanity publishers — says it's a self-publishing company and that it provides self-publishing.

That's not true.

Just as no one can eat lunch for you, no other person or company can self-publish for you. The words just don't make sense.

On the other hand, a "real" self-publisher establishes a business, hires editors and designers, purchases photography, owns ISBNS, obtains LCCNs and copyrights, chooses a printer, and promotes the books.

That's very different from paying for the services of a vanity publisher.

OMG. Outskirts Press actually paid money to distribute a press release. What's next: a cure for the common cold or peace in the Middle-East?

Hmm. Is Outskirts Press paying attention to me?

In the past I slammed the sleazy, incompetent and dishonest vanity publisher for using ineffective freebie press release distribution services to distribute "news" about both Outskirts and its author/victims' books.

Unlike the paid-for services, the freebie services get little attention from the news media they are aimed at, and they even carry ads for competitors of Outskirts and its authors.

Today, a press release from Outskirts announced that its books can be made available on Espresso Book Machines (just like hundreds of thousands of books from other publishers).

It's not surprising that Outskirts is doing this, because Outskirts uses Lightning Source to print books, and Lightning Source feeds book files to Espresso so books can be instantly printed by Espresso vending machines around the world.

What is surprising is that Outskirts has finally realized that when they spend zero to distribute a press release, they get pretty close to zero media coverage.

Amazingly, Outskirts actually shelled out at least $80 to tell the world about their latest news.

Of course, this change doesn't mean that Outskirts is making progress in other areas.

The press release continues the Outskirts Press tradition of bad writing, using the childish phrase "exact same."

The press release continues the Outskirts Press tradition of misleading potential customers. It says, "participation does not require any new processes or publishing 'tools' to master. We take care of all the details." The details consist of Outskirts authorizing Lightning Source to upload files to Espresso — not exactly high-tech "tools to master."

At the time that the press release was distributed, the Outskirts Press website had absolutely nothing about the program, including its cost to authors. A search for "Espresso" on the Outskirts site came up with "no pages found." (Authors who self-publish through Lightning Source but do not use Outskirts, pay nothing for Espresso availability.)

As usual, Outskirts is dishonest. The press release serves up a big bucket of steaming, stinking bullshit about Outskirts being the "leading self-publishing company." Outskirts is not a self-publishing company — either leading or following. Outskirts press is a vanity publisher that turns out some really crappy books promoted with really crappy press releases.

As recently as yesterday Outskirts Press continued to use poorly written ("most recent book to date") and cliche-ridden ("Deftly constructed at 202 pages") freebie press releases to announce the books written by its customers.

Outskirts is now willing to spend money for self-promotion press releases, but not for press releases that promote the authors who pay Outskirts.

Selling what doesn't exist (part 2)

I've said that the term "self-publishing company" makes no sense because no company or person can self-publish you, or self-publish for you — just as no one else can eat lunch for you, take medicine for you or commit suicide for you. That last example got me thinking. I decided to try to come up with a list of phrases that begin with "self" to see if *any* of them could be done for you by another person or business.

- No one can self-immolate you.
- No one can self-destruct you.
- No one can self-medicate you.
- No one can self-educate you.
- No one can self-heal you.
- No one can self-help you.
- No one can self-direct you.
- No one can self-appoint you.
- No one can self-start you.
- No one can self-deprecate you.
- No one can self-express you.
- No one can self-insure you.
- **No one can self-publish you. The words just don't make sense!**

Chapter 15 (1/6/10)
Pathetically stupid Outskirts Press misspelled its own name and helps its competitors

PRLog Free Press Release

Home | Latest Press Releases | Submit Press Releases
PR Home | News Archive | By Category | By Location | By Date

Outskirt Press Announces Tenderhe Darnell V. Neal.

Outskirts Press, Inc. has published Tenderheaded: A Saga of Plai
V. Neal, which is the author's most recent book to date.

FOR IMMEDIATE RELEASE

PR Log (Press Release) – Jan 04, 2010 – Outskirts Press, Inc. has publis
of Plaits and Beads by Darnell V. Neal, which is the author's
most recent book to date. The 6 x 9 Paperback cream in the
POETRY / General category is available worldwide on book
retailer websites such as Amazon and Barnes & Noble for a
suggested retail price of $10.95. The webpage at
www.outskirtspress.com/tenderheaded was launched
simultaneously with the book's publication.

Tate I
Blog v
author
more t
www.tate

Self-P
Book:
Creat

About the Book (Excerpts & Info)

I've come to expect that a press release from Out-skirt**S** Press will include ads for competitors, overused phrases and strange terminology. But this is the first time I've known the Outskirt**S** idiots to *misspell the name of their own company!*

If the company's "infrastructure of talented publish-ing artisans" (and a boss and boss's wife who allegedly majored in English in college) didn't notice that the last letter of their company name was missing from the title of a press release, what are the chances of them publish-ing a proper book?

There's probably no chance at all.

(And like all Outskirt**S** books, this one is deftly con-structed of Paperback cream, is being aggressively pro-moted with pervasive online availability, was published simultaneously with the launch of a webpage [*sic*], claims that an author's first book is his latest book, meets con-sumer demand, and can be ordered for the maximum price set by the author.)

If you have any doubts about Outskirt**S** Press, the company wants you to know that "Outskirt**S** Press represents the future of book publishing, today."

Uh-oh.

Maybe it's time to melt-down the printing presses. When prehistoric publishers had to chisel each word onto the wall of a cave, maybe they were more careful than the staff at Outskirt Pres.

Save up to $199. Write your own Outskirts Press press release

Outskirts Press charges its customer/victims $99 or $199 to produce a crappy press release to announce their new books.

I am pleased to offer a **FREE do-it-yourself Outskirts Press press release template.** All you have to do is fill in a few specifics about your book, copy and paste the completed document onto the website of a freebie news distribution service such as PR.com or PR Log, and you will have achieved everything that Outskirts would charge you for.

Just replace the boldface words below with information about your own book.

Outskirts Press Announces **Oedipus Rex,** the Latest Book from **Athens, Greece** Author **Sophocles**

Athens, Greece, January 07, 429 BCE — (PR.com) — Outskirts Press, Inc. has published **Oedipus Rex** by

71

Sophocles, which is the author's most recent book to date. The 6 x 9 paperback cream in the **Fiction/Tragedy** category is available worldwide on book retailer websites such as Amazon and Barnes & Noble for a suggested retail price of **$14.95.** The webpage at **www.outskirtspress.com/oedipus** was launched simultaneously with the book's publication.

About the Book (Excerpts & Info)

Oedipus Rex is an epic story that examines the constant battle between **parent and child.**

The main character, Oedipus, is the son of King Laius and Queen Jocasta of Thebes. After Laius learns from an oracle that he will be killed by his son, he orders Jocasta to kill the infant Oedipus. Jocasta then orders a servant to do the killing, but the servant abandons the baby in a field, leaving the baby's fate to the gods.

A shepherd rescues the infant and gives it to another shepherd who takes the baby to Corinth, where Oedipus is taken in and raised in the court of the childless King Polybus as if he were his own son.

As a young man, Oedipus hears a rumor that he is not the biological son of Polybus and his wife Merope. When Oedipus asks them, they deny it, but he is still suspicious and he asks the Delphic Oracle who his parents really are. The Oracle seems to ignore this question, telling him instead that he is destined to have sex with his mother and kill his father. Desperate to avoid this horrible fate, Oedipus leaves Corinth in the belief that Polybus and Merope

are indeed his true parents and that if he stays away from them, the prediction can't come true.

On the road to Thebes, he meets Laius, his true father. Unaware of each other's identities, they quarrel over whose chariot has the right-of-way. King Laius tries to hit the insolent youth with his sceptre, but Oedipus knocks him off the chariot and kills him, fulfilling part of the oracle's prophecy.

Shortly after, Oedipus solves the baffling riddle of the Sphinx: "What is the creature that walks on four legs in the morning, two legs at noon, and three in the evening?" People who can't answer, are killed.

Oedipus replies, "Man" (who crawls on all fours as an infant, walks upright later, and needs a walking stick in old age), and the frustrated Sphinx throws herself off a cliff.

Oedipus's reward for answering the riddle and freeing Thebes from her curse is the kingship of Thebes and marriage to Queen Jocasta, his widowed biological mother. He has sex with her and the prophecy is fulfilled, although the main characters don't know it.

Jocasta has children with Oedipus (his daughters are his sisters, his sons are his brothers, his uncle is his brother-in-law). Eventually the family history becomes known. Jocasta hangs herself, and then Oedipus removes the long gold pins that held her dress together, sticks them into his eyes and begs to be exiled.

Deftly constructed at 169 pages, **Oedipus Rex is** being aggressively promoted to appropriate markets with a focus on the **Fiction/Tragedy** category. With U.S. wholesale distribution through Ingram and Baker & Taylor, and pervasive online availability through Amazon, Barnes & Noble and elsewhere, **Oedipus Rex** meets consumer demand through both retail and library markets with a suggested retail price of **$14.95**.

Additionally, **Oedipus Rex** can be ordered by retailers or wholesalers for the maximum trade discount price set by the author in quantities of ten or more from the Outskirts Press wholesale online bookstore at **www.outskirtspress.com/buybooks**.

(Plot summary adapted from Wikipedia)

Chapter 17 (1/28/10)
Suffering from ED?
Outskirts idiots misspell their own name again.

Outsk̲irts Press books can now be ava
the iPhone, currently one of the hotte
Edition option, Outsk̲irt Press is able t
services so that Outsk̲irt Press books
and iPod Touch as well as through Am

In an earlier chapter I showed you a press release from Outskirts Press that left the final "S" off Outskirts.

They've done it again, but this time they misspelled "Outskirts" TWICE in one paragraph.

Is Outskirts Press suffering from Performance Anxiety, or Editorial Dysfunction?

Are the highly touted Outskirts Press "infrastructure of talented publishing artisans" and "veritable army of publishing professionals" nervous and getting sloppier just because they know they're being watched?

If the company's talented infrastructure and veritable army (and a boss and boss's wife who allegedly majored in English in college) didn't notice that the last letter of their company name was missing at least THREE TIMES in press releases, what are the chances of them publishing a proper book?

There's probably no chance at all.

In his blog, Outskirts boss Brent Sampson recently said, "This allows me an opportunity to stress the importance of professional copyediting when publishing a book."

Yeah, right. What about copyediting press releases?

Brent brags that "Our publishing guide *Self-Publishing Simplified* continues to serve as a product brochure, an example of the company's exemplary quality, and evidence that publishing a print-on-demand book does not require an outlandish retail price. Try to find a new book by any other print-on-demand publisher on Amazon for $5.95! The power of our pricing speaks for itself."

Yeah, right.

This inaccurate and dishonest book ("an example of the company's exemplary quality") is priced low because it is an *advertisement* and Brent wants to make it easy for potential customers (i.e., victims) to afford it. It's not priced like a real book that is expected to make money for its author.

Several booksellers offer it (new) for just $2. That price is probably a better indicator of its value.

Chapter 18 (1/29/09)
Michael and Brent debate (sort of)

Brent Sampson, the often-inept boss of often-inept vanity publisher Outskirts Press, blogged about what he perceives to be the difference between "self publishing" and a "self publishing company."

Many people assume that pay-to-publish companies like Outskirts describe their businesses as "self-publishing" in order to cash-in on a term that is exciting, modern, glamorous, revolutionary, hip, cool, in vogue, a buzzword, etc.

- Brent denies that. Instead, he indicates that "self-publishing" has *negative* implications and is used like a warning, to let would-be authors know that the "self-publishing companies" won't do all that is required to make a book a success, and that authors are largely responsible for their book's success or failure.

- I think Brent is being dishonest, and that he uses the "self-publishing" term to attract customers — not to warn them.

BS   I would like to address a point of contention and misunderstanding facing the author-supported self-publishing industry today, and that is the chasm between "self-publishing" and "self-publishing companies" or what some call "vanity" publishing. Authors who have traditionally published books or independently published their own books by doing all the work themselves often denounce "self-publishing companies" as either "vanity" publishers if they're being nice, or "scams" if they're feeling particularly hostile.

MNM   It's more likely that they're trying to warn people.

BS   Neither term is accurate; although I can appreciate their point of view — they've worked hard to accomplish something that self-publishing companies make relatively easy, so you can't blame them for being mad.

MNM   While we critics are upset, we are not yet foaming at the mouth like mad dogs. Except for a small book business that's owned by a self-publishing author, there's no such thing as a "self-publishing company." The words don't make sense the way you and your competitors like Author Solutions use them.

A person can be self-educated, but only if she educated herself. And just as it's impossible for someone else to self-educate you, self-immolate you, self-medicate you, self-express you or self-anything-else you... no other person or company can self-publish you. The words just don't make sense. If others do it to you or for you, you're not doing it yourSELF.

Vanity publishing and self-publishing are as different as murder is from suicide, as different as adoption is from conceiving and giving birth, as different as buying a term paper is from researching and writing one, as different as buying a house is from designing and building one, or paying for a bus ride vs. learning how to drive and driving yourself, or buying a McDonalds Filet-O-Fish vs. catching and cooking a fish.

Publishing is a business where the end-product is a collection of words, and people in the business should use words properly. Brent, I don't expect you to refer to your company as a vanity publisher or even a pay-to-publish company, but you could legitimately call it an author services company. No way in hell is it a self-publishing company.

BS   Ultimately, much of the confusion

MNM   REAL self-publishers aren't confused, but your customers are.

BS   comes down to semantics, and a misunderstanding of what differentiates "self-publishing" from a "self-publishing company." I imagine "self-publishing companies" may use the term "self-publishing" in their marketing efforts, not to anger independent self-publishers, but rather to SET THE EXPECTATIONS of their own authors.

MNM   Oh, come on, Brent. This is the place for facts, not what you *imagine may* be happening. Be honest. Tell the world why YOUR company uses the term. If you are really using the term "self-publishing" to reduce the expectations of potential customers, the term belongs in the fine print of contracts — not in the headlines of ads. You know damn well that you use the term to attract customers — NOT to warn them.

BS   By labeling services as "self-publishing" there is

an attempt to make it clear to the authors who use such services that their success rests largely on their own shoulders,

MNM   Get real. The term is used to glamorize sleazy businesses by deceiving potential customers.

BS   just as it does for authors who independently self-publish.

MNM   NO. Your customers are less likely to succeed compared to skilled and knowledgeable real self-publishers because your books are often poorly edited and poorly promoted — and I have email from your customers and actual Outskirts books and press releases to prove it.

BS   The difference is that with self-publishing companies, instead of incurring the time and effort of establishing a DBA

MNM   It took me less than five minutes and cost me just $8, and my DBA is valid for life!

BS   and or LLC or C-Corp or S-Corp or sole proprietorship with the state,

MNM   NONE of that is necessary for self-publishing

BS   reviewing cover designers,

MNM   Yes of course — that's how to get a good-looking cover.

BS   seeking interior formatters,

MNM   Not difficult.

BS   getting bids from printers,

MNM   Not necessary.

BS   acquiring ISBNs

MNM   Very easy.

BS   dealing with Ingram,

MNM   Not necessary.

BS   dealing with fulfillment,

MNM   Not necessary

BS   dealing with returns,

MNM   Not necessary.

BS   dealing with accounts receivables,

MNM   Not necessary.

BS   dealing with taxes,

MNM   Paying income tax is no different with self-publishing or vanity publishing. You deduct the costs of doing business, and pay tax on the net income.

BS   etc., etc., etc.

MNM   No etceteras.

BS   the author is incurring a service charge and having all those details taken care of for them.

MNM   Oops. "Author" is a single noun. "Them" does not agree with it. Brent, you were an English major in college, weren't you? But, more importantly, Outskirts Press does not take care of all of the details, because with Outskirts Press, editing is an **option**, not a basic part of the publishing packages.

BS   It's not right for everyone, but it is right for a lot of people.

MNM   Crappy books are not right for **any** people.

BS   There are

MNM   Should be "is."

BS   a growing number of companies in the "self publishing" industry.

MNM   Sure — it's the scam *du jour.*

BS   And why not? As the traditional publishing industry continues to struggle, the self-publishing industry is growing at a steady pace and is earning more respectability daily.

MNM   Self-publishing, yes; vanity publishing, no.

BS   The internet has made it possible for anyone to sell a book globally (on sites like Amazon and Barnes & Noble) and has also improved the book marketing reach of authors who leverage popular sites like YouTube and twitter.

MNM   Actually, it's "Twitter."

BS   Very soon, traditional and bestselling authors with established names (Stephen King, Stephanie Meyer, etc.)

MNM   Stephenie!!!

BS   will realize they no longer need traditional publishers and will turn to "self publishing companies"

MNM   Which do not exist.

BS   for a greater stake of the profits.

MNM   That should be "share," not "stake. While Stephen and Stephanie may turn to self-publishing, it seems highly unlikely that they will use a company like Outskirts Press. If they want more money, they may follow the pattern of Hollywood stars who formed their own movie production and distribution companies.

BS   "Self-publishing companies"

MNM   Which do not exist.

BS   are service companies

MNM   Correct — so call them author service companies.

BS   who

MNM   Should be "which."

BS   provide valuable (and convenient) services to writers for a fee. This is no different from any other service industry. For example, I can either choose to do my own taxes, or I can pay H&R Block to do them for me.

MNM   But H. & R. Block doesn't call itself a *self*-tax-preparation company!

BS   I can either build my own house, or I can buy one that has been built by professionals, so I'm confident it won't fall apart.

MNM   What about vanity books that fall apart, or have blobs of glue on the first and last pages, or mis-aligned pages, or defective formatting, or no fact-checking or editing?

BS   I can either milk my own cow, or I can go to 7-11 and buy a gallon of milk that is ready to drink. Are people surprised that 7-11 charges money for milk? Do they get upset that 7-11 charges more money for a gallon of milk than King Soopers [a super market chain in the Rocky Mountains] does? Rational people realize that convenience costs money and that industry know-how costs money.

MNM   Some Outskirts books indicate that your company has inadequate knowhow.

BS   To suggest that a company cannot help you self-publish

MNM   There's nothing wrong with helping someone to self-publish, but Outskirts customers are NOT self-publishing. If Outskirts is the publisher, its authors are NOT self-publishing. If the ISBN and logo on a book indicate that Outskirts is the publisher, the author is NOT the publisher and self-publishing did NOT occur.

BS   is like saying H&R Block cannot help you do your personal taxes

MNM   But H. & R. Block doesn't call itself a *self*-tax-preparation company! Quicken's TurboTax is for people who want to self-prepare their income taxes.

BS   Do I really want to spend my valuable time doing taxes, building a house or milking a cow — all of which first requires [sic] me to LEARN how to properly do all those things? Or would I rather calculate my own hourly rate and determine that it is more cost-effective to pay an expert to do it for me so I can spend my time doing things that are more important to me — like going to work and spending time with my family?

MNM   Brent, some people actually *like* to learn. Some people actually *like* the work involved in self-publishing. It's certainly more fun than doing taxes or milking cows.

BS   Self-publishing companies don't do anything that someone who is very motivated cannot do themselves [*sic*] with a lot of industry knowledge, effort, resources, time, and money.

MNM   It's not a lot of money. It can be done for $600-$1200.

BS   But much like doing taxes, building a house, and yes, even milking a cow, what seems easy at first is actually more complicated than you might expect — I would imagine.

MNM   IMAGINE? Brent, when you are discussing something important, you should not be imagining. This is not the time to imagine what the other side thinks or does. You could ask what it's like to self-publish, read a book about it, or even try it yourself. You've been complaining about how difficult it is to self-publish, but it's very obvious that you don't really know what it's like. All you do is imagine. That's not good enough to make a convincing argument.

BS   Personally, I don't do my own taxes, build my own homes, OR milk cows for my own milk.

MNM   Maybe you should try it, Brent. You might find that you enjoy it. You might get a house you like better, and milk you like better.

BS   Like most people, I pay professionals to do all those things for me. For those authors out there who have already invested their time and energy on the steep learning curve

MNM   It's not very steep. It can be learned in a few days to a few weeks.

BS   that is "self-publishing," naturally they don't see the benefit of using a "self-publishing company."

MNM   Which does not exist.

BS   But most people have better things to do, or at least, their interests lie elsewhere — most people just want to be published authors,

MNM   Most people who want to be published authors want to have good books, and your company turns out some terrible books — including one you wrote.

BS   not publishers.

MNM   If most people *don't* want to be publishers, why do you advertise "Self-*Publish* Your Work. Self-*Publish* from $199?" It sure seems like you are soliciting business from people who *do* want to be publishers. And why are you heading your ads with the phrase that you said lets writers know that they'll have to do a lot of work? If you've being truthful about your use of the term, then your advertising is *very* wrong. It's like putting the cancer warning in big type on the top of a cigarette ad.

BS   You know what they say about the lawyer who represents himself, or the doctor who has herself as a patient, right? The same could be said for most authors. Sure, there are exceptions, but the services of "self publishing companies" are intended for the majority of writers, entrepreneurs and professionals out there who would find value in having a published book, but also value their time enough to let the professionals do it for them.

MNM   Tragically, a huge number of the books published by Outskirts and its competitors are terribly produced and inadequately promoted by "professionals" who don't seem to care about the quality of their work, and don't respond to customers' questions and complaints.

BS   And there's nothing wrong with that. What is wrong is wanting desperately to be published and not doing anything about it — out of fear of failure or fear of someone else telling you that you made "a wrong choice." The only truly wrong choice is not doing anything. As Wayne Gretzky says, "You miss 100% of the shots you don't take."

MNM   And you may miss 100% of the money paid to a vanity publisher.

Chapter 19 (2/4/10)
I'm not sure if Outskirts is cheating or stupid, but I know it's lying.

Inc. 500

©PRWeb®

Inc. 500 Names Outskirts Press Fastest-Growing Self Publishing Company

Denver, CO (PRWEB) August 26, 2009 -- Inc Magazine released their annual Inc 500 list of the nation's fastest-growing companies on Wednesday, August 12. One self-publishing company topped them in the Consumer Products & Services category, made the top 500 -- Outskirts Press.

The annual ranking is based upon the rate of each company's revenue growth from 2005 through 2008. In that span of time, Outskirts Press grew at a rate of 850.5%, making it the fastest growing self-publishing and book marketing company and #268 among all American businesses. Outskirts Press is the 21st fastest-growing business in the Consumer Products & Services category.

In its September 2009 issue, *Inc* magazine named Outskirts Press to its annual "*Inc* 500" list of the nation's fastest-growing privately-held businesses. The ranking is based on the rate of revenue growth from 2005 through 2008, when Outskirts Press claims it grew by 850.5%.

Outskirts Press is the 21st fastest-growing business in the Consumer Products & Services category on the *Inc* list. Companies choose categories to compete in.

Book publishing does not seem to be a genuine consumer product or service like laundry detergent, fast food, DVD rental or shoe repair.

• If Outskirts Press was included in the Business Services category (like others in the publishing business) its rank would drop from #21 to #43. Clearly Outskirts' bragging rights would suffer if it was in the business products category, where it seems to belong.

• However, if Outskirts was listed in the Media category (with others in the publishing business), it would rank #8. The publicity-hungry vanity press could have claimed to be in the TOP TEN, but they goofed by choosing a classification that placed them 13 positions lower, and out of the TOP TEN in a class.

So, did Outskirts choose its category because it expected to gain an unfair advantage over other companies, or just because it's stupid?

The company is often both.

A bit more analysis:

Outskirts Press does a huge amount of self-promotion, often through ineffective freebie press release distribution services.

An Outskirts Press press release writer (probably Jeanine Sampson or Kelly Schuknecht) wants the world to know that *Inc* magazine declared Outskirts to be the "Fastest-Growing Self Publishing Company."

Forget for just a moment that Outskirts is not a self-publishing company.

The release stupidly says: "sales of self-publishing books climbed 132% while the sales of traditionally published books fell by 3%."

"Self-publishing books" would be books about self-publishing, just as running books are about running. The release should have said "self-published" books.

Even worse, Outskirts is seriously distorting the statistics (originally provided by R. R. Bowker). The 132% growth was for on-demand books, which include much more than self-published books. Major traditional publishing companies print-on-demand, as do university presses, vanity presses, and real self-publishers.

➜ Here's the actual statement from Bowker: "Bowker projects that 285,394 On Demand books were produced last year, a staggering 132% increase over last year's final total of 123,276 titles."

The press release about the *Inc* 500 status says that from 2005 through 2008, "Outskirts Press grew at a rate of 850.5%, making it the fastest growing self-publishing and book marketing company and #268 among all American businesses."

That's a bunch of crap!

In truth, Outskirts Press might be #268 among the businesses *that submitted information to the magazine.* But only the IRS has the data to judge revenue growth of "all American businesses." And companies can lie to both the IRS and to *Inc.*

The Outskirts Press company profile published by *Inc* says that Outskirts has just three employees. The

Outskirts website shows three employees (all named Sampson.)

Judging by the poor quality of the company's output, those three people must be terribly overworked and/or terribly unqualified for their jobs.

With about $5 million in annual sales, I'd think the Sampson clan could afford a nice office — but the mailing address for the company is a private mailbox at a UPS Store in Parker Colorado.

Brent and his family probably work at home in their underwear or pajamas. At least they don't spend much money on commuting. How green!

Director of Author Support Kelly Schuknecht lives in Iowa. She probably doesn't commute to Colorado.

It doesn't get much better than this: vanity publisher Outskirts Press brags about its vanity award from a scam organization

An Outskirts Press press release says: "Outskirts Press, Inc. Receives 2009 Best of Business Award. Small Business Commerce Association's Award Honors the Achievement."

"Outskirts Press, Inc. has been selected for the 2009 Best of Business Award in the Publishing category by the Small Business Commerce Association (SBCA)."

That's *not* true. The default award is for "business services." There is no publishing category. Outskirts could have typed in street sweeping, prostitution, burglary, heart surgery or anything.

Basically, the Small Business Commerce Association poses as a national version of your local Chamber of Commerce. However, its main agenda is to sell awards to enhance the walls, tables and egos of its honorees.

Last fall, yours truly received email for AbleComm (my full-time business) saying:

"The Small Business Commerce Association (SBCA) is pleased to announce that AbleComm Inc has been selected for the 2009 Best of Business Award in the Business Services category. The SBCA Best of Business Award Program recognizes the best of small businesses throughout the country. Using consumer feedback and other research, the SBCA identifies companies that we believe have demonstrated what makes small businesses a vital part of the American economy. The selection committee chooses the award winners from nominees based off information taken from monthly surveys administered by the SBCA, a review of consumer rankings, and other consumer reports. Award winners are a valuable asset to their community and exemplify what makes small businesses great. A copy of the press release is available on the SBCA awards website listed below. SBCA herby grants AbleComm Inc a non-exclusive, revocable, license to use, copy, publish, stream, publicly display, reformat, excerpt, and distribute this press release. If you desire, a 2009 Best of Business Award has been designed for your place of business and can be obtained by pressing the receive awards tab while retrieving your press release from the SBCA awards website. Additionally, a Web Logo proclaiming your 2009 Best of Business Award selection can be obtained through our website as well."

I had my choice of paying $57.57 for a plaque, $117.97 for a trophy, or $157.97 for both. The Outskirts press release shows a trophy design copied from the SBCA website, so Outskirts may not have actually spent any money for a physical trophy.

Just as inept Outskirts picked the wrong category for its *Inc* 500 award, it foolishly accepted its little hometown of Parker, Colorado to be displayed on the trophy.

For the same price, instead of being the best publisher in Parker, Outskirts could have displayed a phony award that proclaims it to be the best in Colorado, in the United States, on the planet Earth or in the entire Milky Way Galaxy!

What follows is from
The Better Business Bureau

Recent emails notifying businesses that they have won "prestigious awards" from a national association appear to be part of a widespread scheme designed to get companies to pay for "vanity" awards and plaques. Once the award code is entered into the organization's website, it is revealed that in order to receive this award the business must pay $57.00 to $150.00.

BBB has requested basic information from this company and has received no response. Specifically, BBB asked what publication or places were the award winners displayed and why it is not stated in the email to the businesses that they must pay for their award.

Among the winners were a discount driving school in Maryland, a tattoo removal clinic in California, a bagpipe player in Arizona and a "laser tag family fun center" in Louisiana. Other award winners were in categories such as "astrologers," "disc jockeys," "tanning salons," and "artificial waterfalls."

—

PS: The number of news media that published the Outskirts press release is ONE.

Oops! I'm sorry, folks, but the number should probably be ZERO.

That alleged news medium that published the press release, called *Self Publishing News*, is actually a blog produced by Outskirts Press.

So, we have **a vanity publisher, using its own vanity blog to publish a vanity press release bragging about a vanity trophy**. I couldn't make this up.

When I was notified that my own company was a winner, I created a customized trophy with the geographic area expanded from my city to the entire country.

I also did an award for HBO's Tony Soprano, recognizing his business services in "New Joisey." I think Tony deserves an award more than Outskirts Press does.

Are they part of the Outskirts Press "veritable army of publishing professionals" and "infrastructure of talented publishing artisans?"

There's no need for Outskirts to buy or rent an office when it can rent a mailbox from UPS and let everyone work at home.

Are key employees at Outskirts Press trying to find new jobs?

Some people still use newspapers for job hunting, but more and more use Internet services. **Linkedin** is an on-line social network of over 55 million "experienced professionals" from 150 industries and 200 countries.

One stated objective is to help members to "Discover inside connections that can help you land jobs..."

It appears that the two key people at Outskirts Press who are not members of the Sampson family are ready to jump off the sleazy ship as soon as they get suitable offers.

The Outskirts Press Manager of Author Services Karl Schroeder says he is interested in career opportunities, job inquiries, new ventures, business deals and consulting offers.

Director of Author Support Kelly Schuknecht wants to hear about job inquiries and business deals.

Based on Karl's terrible arithmetic and Kelly's terrible writing, I would not hire them to publish toilet paper.

Actually, some Outskirts Press books are better suited to wiping than reading.

ADVICE TO JOB SEEKERS:

1.   If you're looking for a new job, try not to publicize your desire where your current employer can find it. Disloyalty may be a reason for dismissal.

2.   Your chance of landing a better job is severely limited if potential employers can easily find examples of your substandard work.

Chapter 22 (2/9/2010)
Reality Check: Outskirts Press's distribution vs. real self-publishing

Outskirts Press frequently brags and lies to make it seem like it has advantages over other paths to publication — particularly independent (i.e., "real") self-publishing.

In an effort to get customers, Outskirts boss Brent Sampson has written many sentences on the company website and in his blog and books that are simply not true. He wrote, "The majority of independently self-published authors find it nearly impossible to secure distribution through book wholesalers like Ingram and Baker & Taylor."

In reality, Brent has no way of knowing the experiences of the majority of independently self-published authors. It's highly likely that those people (which include me) have their books printed by Lightning Source, which provides automatic access to Ingram and Baker & Taylor. It's nearly impossible *not* to secure distribution.

Brent also says, "One of the most common misconceptions about print-on-demand companies [euphemism for "vanity publishers"] is that their only value is printing books one at a time. While it is true that just-in-time printing is an advantage of publishing with a POD publishing service company, there are many greater advantages than just printing. Perhaps the best reason of all, however, is not the printing of the books, but the distribution of the books after publication."

That's more B.S. from **B**rent **S**ampson.

Below is the distribution diagram for the more-expensive Outskirts Press Diamond, Ruby, and Pearl publishing packages:

What follows is a modification of the Outskirts Press chart that shows how distribution works if you are a real self-publisher and have your books printed by Lightning Source. All you lose are direct sales from the Outskirts Press website (which are probably insignificant). If you form your own little publishing company, you'll probably publish faster, get your money faster, and make more money. If you publish properly, you should have better books and have a better chance of getting your books reviewed.

Outskirts website stupidity:

"All Ruby books include ... wholesale distribution via Ingram, Baker & Taylor, Amazon, Barnes & Noble, and elsewhere."

Amazon and Barnes & Noble are book retailers — *not* wholesale distributors. A publisher should know this.

Chapter 23 (2/28/09)
OMG, another brain fart from Brent Sampson

Brent Sampson and his Outskirts Press are notorious for making stupid mistakes. I am becoming notorious for pointing them out.

In a recent blog, Brent wrote: "Well, this consideration revolves around SEO, which will be a common topic of this blog. At Outskirts Press we've always been somewhat cognizant of SEO, and in 2010 we are really accelerating those efforts because, frankly, we've hit something of a glass ceiling with the ROI on PPC. How's that for an acronym filled paragraph?"

Sorry, Brent, but it's not an "acronym filled paragraph" (or an acronym-filled paragraph).

Brent claims to have majored in English at the University of Colorado. Apparently he missed the class that dealt with acronyms.

An acronym is an abbreviation that is *pronounced like a word*. Examples include scuba, laser, AIDS, IKEA, NATO and ACORN.

"SEO" is the abbreviation for Search Engine Optimization. It's pronounced "ess-ee-oh."

If it was an acronym, it would be pronounced "see-oh."

"ROI" is the abbreviation for Return On Investment. It's pronounced "are-oh-eye."

If it was an acronym, it would be pronounced like the first name of Roy Rogers, king of the cowboys (above, with his "queen," Dale Evans.)

"PPC" is the abbreviation for Pay Per Click. It's pronounced "pee-pee-see."

If it was an acronym, it might be pronounced "peepk" or "pipick."

Brent once told the world that "Errors in your writing cause readers to question your credibility." He's absolutely right.

Chapter 24
OMG, another complaint from an Outskirts author

Posted by "Mark" in selfpublishingreview.com

Be forewarned folks. I am in the middle of getting a book published by Outskirts Press and it is a horrible experience. Their customer service is truly the worst. They have deep systemic issues and nickel and dime you to death — and I bought the highest priced package they have!!

They deliberately do not publish any names other than your "author rep" so that you have no recourse trying to call someone in management. Even their phone number ensures you cannot access anyone.

I have noted 26 major failings so far including gross failure to communicate. They only send email and do not respond to phone calls nor will they ever call you. Adds a terrible time delay and burdensome communication style when problems or issues arise.

The person who is your rep has no authority. Everyone associated with the actual work does it behind a barrier with him/her in the middle. No one does anything directly, it is all sent out. Like having to tell one person, who then tells another, who then passes it along. By the time you get something back it is a mess. [They] could not solve simple problems.

Wanted some simple black and white photos included in a how-to book. They kept rejecting what I sent with little guidance as to how to solve the problem. After I sent a 1200 dpi copy, they still could not agree to use it but could not provide what they needed other than to continuously send their submission guidelines several times. (Written for techies, too).

Several other publishing companies offered solutions but not Outskirts Press. They had no clue and could not have the simple courtesy of calling to try and solve the problem. Time lost? 8 weeks. You pay for an item, say 10 photos, and submit 6. But then you try to submit more photos and they say you must buy another 10 — you cannot use the leftovers. This is not written anywhere either.

Can you sense my frustration? I could go on but let this be a warning. Their website, which is full of copy errors (!!!) looks pretty but the place is only good if you personally enjoy being totally frustrated many times over.

PS. they are consummately polite. My author rep always maintained her politeness but I have recorded lots of apologies to date with little or no real progress with the associated problems.

Why am I so damned critical?

Any of you who have read more than two or three editions of my blog know that I frequently criticize inept and dishonest vanity publishers and terrible writers.

Pompous incompetents are funny, it's fun to write about them, and I'm performing a public service by exposing them.

I've always liked deflating big egos, and revealing scams. In Hans Christian Andersen's *The Emperor's New Clothes*, I'd be the little kid who yelled out that the idiot ruler was parading in his undies. I have a powerful internal bullshit detector and I am by nature a bit of a wise-ass and seldom hold anything back. I see no need to be nice to jerks with big egos. I am not afraid of being sued, and my wife is so scared of my constant "pushing the limit," that she won't read what I write.

Yesterday I spent two wonderful hours with the man who taught me English and history in seventh grade. I had not spoken with him since June of 1959, so we had a lot to catch up on.

The main reason for my visit was to give him a copy of my book *Stories I'd Tell My Children (but maybe not until they're adults*. The book includes more than 100 mostly hysterically funny (others have said that — not just me) stories that span 55 years. Incompetence is a frequent theme for the stories, and with no specific plan, it appears that I've targeted lots of incompetent doctors, lawyers and teachers.

I had a lot of really lousy teachers, and a few superb ones, including Lawrence DePalma, whom I visited yesterday. In the book, I wrote much more about the bad teachers, both as a warning and because they stimulated writing funny stories.

In the back of the book I have a two-page "honor roll" where I pay tribute to my few good teachers, like "Mr. D," and I wanted him to see it.

Because there are so many stories about bad teachers (and I decided to write the book when I was in sixth grade and the victim of a terrible teacher), I felt the need to point out to Mr. D that I am definitely not anti-teacher. I told him that my mother was a teacher, my father briefly taught college, my sister is a teacher, her husband taught in the same school that Mr. D taught me in, their son is a teacher, and I suppose I think of myself as teaching through my 40-plus years of writing.

While driving away from Mr. D's house, I thought about why I target bad doctors, lawyers and teachers in my book. The answer quickly came to me. It's because these three professions are so important, that when the professionals screw-up, they can do terrible damage.

Doctors are involved with us even when we are still pre-natal. They deliver us to the world, and heal us when we are ill or wounded. Their mission is to preserve life; and when they screw up, people can die.

Teachers are responsible for informing, shaping and directing each new generation of human beings. When a teacher screws up, kids can be misinformed, misshapened and misdirected.

Lawyers are entrusted to protect our rights — while negotiating contracts and defending us in court. As legislators, they make laws, and as judges they rule on cases. When lawyers screw up, people agree to bad deals, children and spouses lose inheritances, guilty people go free, innocent people are executed, and millions suffer because of bad laws.

I can pick out other critical professions and occupations. If architects screw up, buildings fall down. If engineers screw up, airplanes fall down and cellphone batteries overheat. If pharmacists screw up, people can die from taking the wrong medication. If cooks screw up, people can get poisoned. If accountants screw up, their clients pay too much tax, or may get fined. If rulers screw up, their citizens die in the wrong wars. Etc.

When I was the victim of some terrible teachers, I complained to my mother (before she became a teacher). She did not believe my reports of lunacy, incompetence and sadism in the classroom and said that teachers must be respected because of their position regardless of incompetence or derangement.

When we realize that some people in power are not worthy of automatic respect simply because of their title or uniform, some of us become incurable cynics.

I have trouble accepting authority. I know that if I was in the army and my sergeant ordered me to peel potatoes, I'd respond either, "Why should I?" "Get a machine," "Do it yourself," or "Go fuck yourself" — and I'd be in prison or out of the army. Fortunately, I was never in the army.

Vanity publishers probably have not caused deaths like bad doctors or bad judges or bad presidents. But they do cause writers to waste time and money, and cause readers to buy some terrible books. As shelves and websites get clogged with crap, it can be harder for good books to be recognized.

We all choose our battles and our opponents — some puny, some powerful. Ralph Nader fought General Motors. I admire his zeal, although I loved my own 1965 Corvair Corsa. *Consumer Reports* targets dangerous and difficult-to-use products and points out bad values. Thousands of reviewers warn us about bad books, movies and restaurants. My blog often goes after bad publishers and writers (but I have praised good books).

We should all be crusaders. Don't be afraid to call attention to naked emperors, corrupt cops, stupid judges, bad burgers, bad cars, bad books, bad movies, bad bosses, inaccurate articles, and sloppy driveway pavers.

But be equally dedicated to providing praise when deserved.

If you hear a street musician whom you like, don't just dump a quarter in her or his coffee cup and move on. Stick around to dig the performance; and at break time, shake a hand and give some encouragement. If you've enjoyed a good meal in a restaurant, tell the manager (who mostly hears complaints) and go into the kitchen to shake hands with the chef, and write something nice online.

It's important for inept and dishonest people to know that their failures and crimes will be discovered and publicized.

It's equally important for the hard-working good guys to know that their efforts will be recognized and rewarded.

Chapter 26
What would Jesus think?

Christian Publishing Here
www.outskirtspress.com   Fast & easy from $199. Keep your rights.

Full-service Christian publishing
Keep 100% of your rights and 100% of your author royalties

Like some other secular vanity publishers, Outskirts Press advertises that it provides "Christian Publishing," and claims to be "a full-service Christian book publisher."

There doesn't seem to be any official definition of Christian Publishing, but I found a list of Christian Values at The Christian Bible Reference Site.

Outskirts Press doesn't do well:

Be honest: NOPE   Don't be a hypocrite: NO
Be humble: NO WAY   Don't be self-righteous: SORRY
Live a moral life: OOPS   Respect all people: NYET

"Real" Christian publishers generally provide a theological review to ensure that submitted material is theologically sound and is consistent with Christian theology and morality. Outskirts Press does not offer theologically based reviews or editing.

B.S. from Brent Sampson

(Don't believe anything after the first sentence.)

"[Independent self-publishers] pay for each element of production separately, or do all the work themselves. That is bad. Then, when the book is printed, they have to track orders, bill customers, handle fulfillment, and maintain inventory. And that is the best-case scenario, because that means their book is actually selling. It probably isn't. Without any wholesale distribution, the book is likely to end up collecting dust and taking up space in your garage.

Perhaps the worst part is the initial cost. Offset printers expect you to pay for high quantities of books up-front to justify the cost of a print run. In fact, a *Newsweek* article once indicated that an independent self-publishing author should be prepared to spend between $5,000 to [sic] $25,000! That's a lot of money."

Chapter 27
It's not just Outskirts

Vanity publishing is filled with cynics, scoundrels, paranoids, incompetents, hypocrites, slobs and liars. Competitors of Outskirts Press lie and produce poorly written, ugly, overpriced books without professional editing. The books have low sales and seldom get reviewed. Authors are disappointed, embarrassed and furious.

Lulu.com founder Bob Young said, "We publish a huge number of really bad books." If he knows they're  really bad books, he shouldn't publish them. Bob misspelled "misspell" and confused "less" and "fewer." A publisher should know better.

Thomas Nelson Publishers CEO Michael Hyatt has a blog that automatically blocks the comments from people who previously disagreed with him. Nelson has a "Christian" vanity press division that lies about providing self-publishing and free books.

Esquire Publications boss Elva Thompson is a terribly sloppy writer and editor. Someone who purchased a book she edited said, "My five-year-old son could do better. I would not pay her a dollar to publish my books! She has to be one of the most unprofessional women I have ever met."

Who's so vain?

The word "vanity" implies excessive pride in one's appearance, qualities, abilities, achievements and appeal.

Vanity has been considered a sin. It can lead to wasted resources and wasted lives. It can also lead to useful activities and important accomplishments.

Most or all artistic people have some degree of vanity, or they would not produce or perform.

Most people seem to like themselves. There are gradations in vanity, ranging from justified confidence to outrageous, obnoxious egomania.

In *You're So Vain*, Carly Simon wrote and sang that some man (possibly Warren Beatty or Mick Jagger) is so vain that he probably thinks that the song is about him.

Vanity publishers stay in business because vain people are willing to spend money to flatter themselves. A vanity publisher depends on the vanity of writers who strive to become "published authors." Those publishers make most of their money from writers, not from readers.

◆If you work with a vanity publisher, you pay all of the expenses of publishing, and have all of the risks and all of the loss.

◆A book published by a vanity publisher is often assumed to have been rejected as unworthy of publication by traditional publishers.

◆Here's another way of looking at vanity and publishing: Maybe the most vain writers are those who will delay publication for years or decades in hopes of being accepted by a traditional publisher, instead of quickly self-publishing, reaching the public, making their points, and making some money.

Chapter 28
Sifting through the BS:
What is "real" self-publishing?

If you pay money to another company (other than the printer) to manufacture your books, you are NOT a self-publisher but are using a vanity publisher (which may call itself something else). You will probably pay more money, make less money, and wait longer for the books to be available for people to buy. The books may also be so bad that few people will buy them. It's also hard to get reviews for books that carry the labels of a vanity publisher. The essence of being an independent, self-published author is more control, more work, and — with a bit of luck — more income, more satisfaction, and even more fun than if the books were published by another person or company. An independent, self-published author is not just a writer. She or he owns and operates a business.

If I tell people I'm "self-publishing" my books, most of them don't understand what I'm talking about. A few who think they do understand will try to suppress a sneer.

On the other hand, I seem to get much more respect if I say I own a publishing company. It's a true statement. I don't have to point out that I am the sole employee, or that it's only a part-time job and so far it has published only books I've written.

There's no need to divulge that the publishing company is a subsidiary of my primary business in an unrelated field and shares its address. I have business cards that identify me as the publisher of Silver Sands Books, and other cards for other businesses.

At its extreme, the self-publisher will write, edit, design, illustrate, print, bind, promote, sell and ship the books. Most self-publishers are a bit less extreme (and less egomaniacal), and will hire others for editing, designing, illustrating etc.

Bookbinding on the kitchen table is slow and messy. Most independent self-publishers have complete control over their books, but use another company to print and distribute them. Some will pay for specialists in promotion and publicity, or even hire salespeople — but that's uncommon.

There's lots of confusion between self-publishing and "vanity" publishing. Ben Franklin was a self-publisher  and wasn't put down for it. I hope you won't be, either.

For many years there have been ads aimed at writers, with headlines like, "For the writer in search of a publisher," "We want to read your book," "Manuscripts wanted," and "Authors wanted."

The advertisers promise to enable you to become a "published author." The ads are not from traditional publishers or from literary agents, but from vanity publishers

— companies that use the author's money to produce and sell the books.

The requirements for acceptance by a vanity publisher (regardless of the description it uses) are not writing talent and an interesting subject. Usually, all you'll need are blood pressure and a credit card.

There is only one customer a vanity publisher is interested in selling to: the author/customer.

A non-vanity publisher, whether it's a one-person self-publisher or a giant like Random House, hopes to sell books to thousands or millions of readers. Companies like Random House don't have to advertise to attract writers and receive manuscripts.

Sometimes vanity publishers use other terms, including: *subsidy publishing, co-operative publishing, joint venture publishing, POD publishing,* and (most deceptive) *self-publishing.*

The term "vanity publishing" is held in disrepute, and the terms "self-publishing" and "indie publishing" are becoming increasingly respectable, so many of the vanity presses are trying to portray themselves as self-publishers and indie publishers. They're also using another current buzzword to attract customers: Print-On-Demand (POD).

121

If you do a Google search for "self-publishing" you'll get a long list of links plus paid advertisements for companies that want you to think they will help you to self-publish. Most of them will collect between $399 and $10,000 to produce your books.

Vantage Press, in business for over 50 years, now calls itself a "subsidy publisher" (which I think is a misuse of the term), and is refreshingly clear about the financial prospects for its customers. They say, "**Most books by new authors do not sell well, and most authors do not regain the publishing fee**" and "**There is no assurance that your book will be reviewed.**"

On the other hand, they try to scare people considering independent self-publishing by saying, "Self-publication sometimes can be satisfying and profitable. But before embarking on such a venture, ask yourself whether you will have the time to coordinate manufacturing a book, to promote it and advertise it, and to ship, keep records, collect bills, etc."

There is no denying that book promoting is a lot of work, but you can't expect *any* publisher to do all of the promotion for you. If you use a Print-On-Demand printer such as Lightning Source, there's no need to coordinate manufacturing or to ship books or collect bills. Record-keeping is minimal and advertising is optional and can be inexpensive.

In England, Johnathan Clifford leads "a campaign for truth and honesty" about vanity publishing and won a *Daily Mirror* **"Good Service Award"** for protecting the rights of Britain's authors.

Johnathan is credited with having invented the term *vanity publishing* "when two American companies were advertising widely throughout the U.K. offering to publish individual poems in anthologies at £9 and £12 each respectively."

Johnathan warns, "Many unwary authors are encouraged by a vanity publisher's initial promotional material which usually praises the work submitted — whatever its quality. Such publishers often misleadingly refer to themselves as 'partnership,' 'self-,' 'joint venture 'or 'subsidy' publishers. But however they may refer to themselves and however much they may deny that they are — **if they charge you to publish your book, they are a vanity publisher**."

He continues, "A dishonest vanity publisher makes money not by selling copies of a book, but by charging clients as much as possible to print an unspecified number of copies of that book. Some vanity publishers will print as few copies as they feel they can get away with. Most will claim to market their publications. However, major book buyers have gone on record recently stating that they do not buy copies of books centrally from vanity publishers, but only as a result of the effort of the author in that author's local area."

Except for books that appear to be obscene or libelous, a vanity press will generally print anything. Some vanity presses will automatically send an author a letter of praise for a submitted manuscript, even without reading the submission. There have been experiments

123

where intentionally horrible manuscripts were said to have high sales potential, and a book allegedly **written by a dog** was accepted.

Literary agents — who often function as gatekeepers on the road to traditional publishers — typically reject 99% of the book proposals and manuscripts that they receive. Vanity presses, since they make money by selling services to writers rather than by selling books to readers, probably accept 99% (or even 100%) of their submitted manuscripts.

The lack of selectivity is the prime cause of vanity publishing's bad reputation. Even though traditional publishers make many bad guesses (they frequently reject books that become successful with other publishers and accept books that quickly become failures), their selectivity and financial commitment does provide a powerful endorsement for the writers and books they choose to accept.

Some books will never be acceptable to mainstream publishers merely because of limited appeal, regardless of their literary merit. A company that wants to sell tens of thousands of copies of each title will not be interested in a family history, unless it's a very famous family.

Some publishers produce books with little or no literary merit to cash in on a celebrity author or subject.
◆A starlet's name can sell tons of diet books.
◆*I was Oprah's Proctologist* would likely be a bestseller.

124

Vanity publishers exist to feed the egos of — and extract money from — writers who have little or no chance of being a financial success, but are willing to pay money to have books printed with their names on the covers. Their egos are often much larger than their talents. They'll pay money even if it means that no books will ever be sold and most of them will pile up in the garage, rotting away with mildew until they are finally dumped when the author dies or the house is sold.

Print-On-Demand can lower the cost and waste of vanity publishing, but does not change the overriding principle.

Author Mick Rooney says this about vanity publishing: "Vanity, to me, isn't Aunt Maple wanting her life story published, nor is it some spotty college teenager thinking he has written 'The Great American Novel.' It is a publishing business set up to prey upon (writers') naiveté, not their vanity."

"Vanity Publishers," he continues, "operate on the 'bait and snare' model of business. Get the customer interested enough; laud their work to high heaven; demonize traditional publishers; throw a veil of complexity on the publishing process; and like used car salesmen, don't point out the scratches or the cracked chassis or the full costs until the customer asks how much to make the check out for and then hit them over the head with a baseball bat. The vanity lies with the publisher smug and disingenuous enough to keep doing it."

On the other hand, authors who undertake real self-publishing usually have a better chance of financial success. The most successful self-publishers know more about book production and promotion than the customers of vanity presses do. They are willing to work harder

125

and want more control of the final product, faster speed-to-market, and more profit than they would have if they worked through traditional publishers.

They also want to spend less, or at least get more for their money, than if they used a vanity publisher.

What's not really self-publishing?

Despite what you'll read in their ads and promotional literature, if you work with a company like Outskirts Press, AuthorHouse, IUniverse or Xlibris, you are NOT a self-publisher. You are a customer. *They* are the publishers and they will do — or they say they will do — a lot of the work that a true self-publisher does for her- or himself. This is not necessarily bad. Maybe you don't want to have to find someone to design your cover and don't want to deal with printers and hire an editor.

On the other hand, **if you work with these companies, you give up control, speed-to-market, and a big chunk of money.**

You may also end up with a really ugly, error-ridden book that will embarrass you and that no one will buy.

Do readers care who published your book?

Zoe Winters is a romance writer and blogger. She says, "The average reader doesn't care how a book gets to market. If the book is good, it doesn't matter if your Chihuahua published it."

Can you pass the self-publishing test?

You can't be a self-publisher unless you are a publisher. If you expect your business to be recognized as a real publishing company by others in the publishing business, you must "own" the ISBN (International Standard Book Number) that is printed on and in your books.

In North America, ISBNs are assigned by **R. R. Bowker.**

Unless you buy an ISBN from either Bowker or an official Bowker agent, you are simply *not* a publisher. If you're not a publisher, you can't be a self-publisher. You might be an author who pays a company to publish your book; but you are not a self-publisher if the ISBN on your book was assigned to *that* company, not to *your* company.

Another Outskirts Press Author — "Mad as Hell"

One exasperated author whose book was accepted on 10/7/07 only had a defective galley proof on 3/11/08, the date he cancelled his contract. The Outskirts Press contract promises publication (not a defective galley proof) within 90 days. And, the galley copy had 314 mistakes in the first 100 pages.

(from outskirtspressdirtytricks.wordpress.com)

Chapter 29
Editors and Editing

Your book's editor could be — but shouldn't be — you.

Obviously it's important that you read, re-read, and re-read some more to polish your text to near perfection. However, it's a fundamental fact of writing that the creator of the words will never catch all of the errors. You will think you are reading words that are really in your mind and not on the screen or on the paper. You will fall in love with certain words or phrases that are really unlovable. Maybe some words, sentences, paragraphs, or whole chapters should be shifted, shortened, or even completely eliminated. These are choices best left to someone other than the creator.

There are several kinds of editing that can be done by one or more people.

◆**Copyediting** (or "copy editing" or "copy-editing") is looking for and fixing all of the tiny errors that infect every written work. A skilled copyeditor has good vision to spot typographical errors, is an excellent speller and a perfect grammarian. She should have an excellent memory to notice inconsistencies, such as "3 a.m." on one page and "5PM" 100 pages later.

Copyeditors generally follow specific semi-official "styles" for writing, promulgated in such books as *The New York Times Manual of Style and Usage, The Associated Press Stylebook*, and *The Chicago Manual of Style*. The books dictate such things as capitalization, abbreviation, and hyphenation. Sometimes they agree with each other. Sometimes they don't. As editor and publisher, you can set up your own style, and perhaps get help from your copyeditor who may have more sense than you do.

DON'T EVEN DREAM of relying on your spell-checker to do the work of a copyeditor.

Copyediting fees can be based on the size of the work, the time involved, or just a negotiated flat fee. If your book is technical and requires specialized knowledge or familiarity with the subject, expect to pay more.

A typical range is $200 to $1,000. This is not a job for a neighbor or a relative. If you need to save money, see if you can hire an editor from a local newspaper, or even a good college paper, rather than a full-time professional copyeditor. Check references, and read some examples of her or his work.

Copyeditors don't need to be familiar with your subject and may not even need to understand what you are writing about. They work on the micro — not the macro — level.

A word of warning: **no copy editor is perfect**. None will catch every error, and some may actually insert errors where there were none before. Read. Read. Read.

◆**Hard editing** is an effort to actually improve what you've written, not just correct little errors.

After working as a writer and editor for over 40 years, I don't bother paying someone to hard edit my work. However, I do admit that, after seeing my finished books, I sometimes wished that I had someone looking over my shoulder to ask, "Are you sure you want to include that?" or "Is that what you really mean to say?" I initially hired Sheila to copyedit one of my books. She made so many important suggestions and improvements that I "promoted" her to editor.

A copyeditor can work on just a sentence or a paragraph or a chapter, but a hard editor should get to know the entire book before actually editing.

While the hard editor probably won't contribute more than a few words, and is not a co-author, she or he may suggest major changes in structure, particularly rearranging sequences, changing viewpoints (from first-person to third, for example), emphasizing or playing down characters or events, killing or adding material, etc.

A hard editor may be paid by the word, page, hour or project. Typical fees are $25 to $50 per hour, $1,000 per book, or two cents per word. Wordclay charges six cents per word.

You may save money if your hard editor is also your copyeditor, but be careful. The hard editing process may cause errors that copyediting should remove.

◆**Technical editing** is major-league fact-checking, and is not necessary for all books. If your book deals with solar energy, Renaissance art or the Cold War, you'd better hire someone who is highly familiar with photovoltaic efficiency, Michelangelo or the Warsaw Pact, and knows the reliable reference works in the field.

Technical editors don't work only on technical books. They might get involved in cookbooks or historical novels — any book that could be tainted by incorrect information. You can pay a few bucks per page, or hundreds or even thousands of dollars per book.

◆**Proofreading** is not the same as editing, but it's related. At one time, a proofreader would simultaneously view the author's original manuscript and a near-final "proof" provided by the printer. He or she would constantly look from the original to the copy and back to try to spot errors and mark them.

Today, there is little chance of a printer's introducing an error, especially with independent self-publishing where the author produces a PDF that is the source of the printed page. Modern proofreading is usually just the "final inspection" before the printer starts turning out books to be sold.

The author should certainly proofread, but it's a good idea to have at least one additional set of eyes to look over your proofs. Do your best, but don't expect to catch every error. It's extremely unusual for a published book to be error-free. If you strive for absolute perfection, your books will never reach the market. It took me a long time to accept this, and I'll pass along some hard-learned and valuable advice: **Sometimes "good enough" really *is* good enough. At some point you have to let go.** Each revision of your book should get a little closer to perfection.

Another tip: **proofread in multiple formats**: on screen in word-processing, on screen in PDF, in a printout from your PC, and in a bound book from your book printer. Different errors will show up in each format.

Good, inexpensive proofreading can usually be provided for $10 per hour by English majors or journalism majors from a local college.

About the author

Michael N. Marcus is a journalist, author, advertising copywriter, publisher and telecommunications executive.

He provides the words for about 40 websites and blogs, has been an editor at *Rolling Stone* and has written for many other magazines and newspapers.

This is Michael's tenth book, and his third book about publishing. He also writes two blogs about writing and publishing, and is founder and president of the Independent Self-Publishers Alliance. The organization encourages and helps writers to become truly independent self-publishers so they can avoid using vanity publishers.

Born in 1946, Michael's a proud member of the first cohort of the Baby Boom, along with Dolly Parton, Candy Bergen, Donny Trump, Billy Clinton and Georgie Bush.

At the urging of a misguided guidance counselor, he went to Lehigh University to study electrical engineering, and was quickly disappointed to learn that engineering was mostly math. Slide rules were not as much fun as soldering irons, so he became a journalism major and made money editing term papers for future engineers.

Michael lives in Connecticut with his wife, Marilyn, Hunter, their Golden Retriever and a lot of stuff — including both indoor and outdoor telephone booths, a "Lily Tomlin" switchboard, lots of books, CDs and DVDs, and many black boxes with flashing lights. Marilyn is very tolerant.

More: www.MichaelMarc.us

Available at Amazon, Barnes & Noble and other
booksellers.

**the100 Worst
Self-Publishing
Misteaks** *akes*

How amateurs can publish books like professionals
or even better

**Sheila M. Clark
Michael N. Marcus**

Includes Publishing Hall of Shame

Available at Amazon, Barnes & Noble and other booksellers. (Coming in July, 2010.)

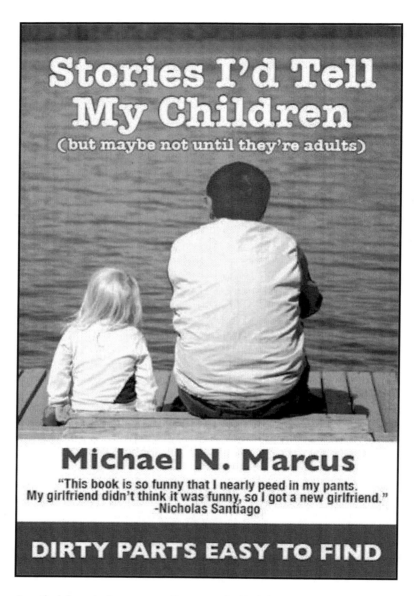

Stories I'd Tell My Children
(but maybe not until they're adults)

Michael N. Marcus

"This book is so funny that I nearly peed in my pants. My girlfriend didn't think it was funny, so I got a new girlfriend."
-Nicholas Santiago

DIRTY PARTS EASY TO FIND

Available at Amazon, Barnes & Noble and other booksellers.

The complete guide to phones, phone systems, phone services and phone accessories

Michael N. Marcus

"I've been in telecommunications for 30 years, but I still learned a lot from this book."
-Fred Marotti, Associated Business Systems

Available at Amazon, Barnes & Noble and other booksellers.